Seasonal
GARDEN IDEAS

EASY PROJECTS FOR THE SMALL GARDEN

Executive Editor	Nick Rowe
Managing Editor	Emily Anderson
Author	Aune Butt
Designer	Graham Meigh
Proof Reader	Marianne Coghlan
Indexer	Aune Butt
Production	Priti Kothary
Special thanks to	Brian Carter

Photographic credits:

Page 4(l) GC/Nicola Stocken Tomkins**, (r)** GC/Andrew Lawson; **5(l)** GC/Liz Eddison, **(r)** PL/GPL/Richard Bloom; **8(l)** GC/Andrew Lawson, **(c)** GC/Liz Eddison**, (r)** PL/GPL/Juliette Wade; **12(l)** GC/Andrew Lawson, **(c)** GC/Nicola Stocken Tomkins**; (r)** Alamy/Paul Thompson; **13(l)** GAP/Brian North, **(tr)** GC/Andrew Lawson, **(bc)** GC/Liz Eddison, **(br)** PL/GPL; **14** GC/Nicola Stocken Tomkins; **16** GC/Michelle Garrett; **18** GC/Nicola Stocken Tomkins; **20** GC/Jonathan Buckley; **22** GC/Andrew Lawson; **24** GC/Nicola Stocken Tomkins; **26** PL/GPL/Howard Rice; **28** GC/Andrew Lawson/Lord Leycester Hospital, Warwick; **30** Harpur Garden Images; **32** GC/Derek Harris; **34** GC/ Andrew Lawson/Design by Mary Keen; **36** GAP/Pernilla Bergdahl; **38** Alamy/Paul Thompson; **40** GC/Neil Sutherland; **42** GAP/Heather Edwards/Design by Michele Fitzsimmons & Sara Bentley; **44** GAP/Brian North; **46** GC/Liz Eddison; **48(l)** GC/Liz Eddison, **(c)** GC/Andrew Lawson, **(br)** GAP/Friedrich Strauss; **49(l)** GC/Nicola Stocken Tomkins**, (tr)** GAP/John Glover, **(bl)** GC/Andrew Lawson, **(br)** Harpur Garden Images; **50** GC/Nicola Stocken Tomkins; **52** GC/Derek Harris; **54** GC/Andrew Lawson; **56** GC/Nicola Stocken Tomkins; **58** GC/Nicola Stocken Tomkins; **60** GC/Liz Eddison; **62** GC/Liz Eddison; **64** GC/Liz Eddison; **66** GC/Liz Eddison; **68** GC/Liz Eddison; **70** GC/Nicola Stocken Tomkins; **72** Harpur Garden Images; **74** Harpur Garden Images; **76** GC/Andrew Lawson; **78** GC/Nicola Stocken Tomkins; **80** GC/Liz Eddison; **82** GC/Andrew Lawson; **84** GC/Liz Eddison; **86** GC/Liz Eddison/Design by Rupert Golby; **88** GC/Andrew Lawson; **90** GC/Andrew Lawson/Design by Dan Pearson; **92** GAP/Friedrich Strauss; **94** GC/Liz Eddison; **96** GAP/John Glover; **98** GC/Marie O'Hara/Penny Smith; **100** GC/Nicola Stocken Tomkins; **102** PL/GPL/Friedrich Strauss; **104** GC/Nicola Stocken Tomkins; **106** GC/Nicola Stocken Tomkins; **108(l)** GC/Liz Eddison, **(c)** GC/Nicolad Stocken Tomkins, **(br)** GC/Gary Rogers; **109(l)** GC/Liz Eddison, **(tr)** GC/Nicola Stocken Tomkins, **(bc)** GC/Derek St Romaine, **(br)** GC/Jonathan Buckley; **110** GAP/Friedrich Strauss; **112** GC/Liz Eddison; **114** GAP/John Glover; **116** GC/Derek Harris; **118** GC/Nicola Stocken Tomkins; **120** PL/GPL/Juliette Wade; **122** GC/Andrew Lawson; **124** GC/Jonathan Buckley; **126** GC/Derek Harris; **128** GC/Liz Eddison; **130** GC/Derek St Romaine; **132** GC/Nicola Stocken Tomkins; **134** GC/Liz Eddison; **136** GC/Nicola Stocken Tomkins; **138** GC/Nicola Stocken Tomkins; **140** GC/Jonathan Buckley/Design by Paul Kelly; **142** GC/Liz Eddison/Design by Helen Williams/RHS Hampton Court 2008; **144** Alamy/Mammalpix; **146** GC/Gary Rogers/Design by Geoffrey Whie, RHS Chelsea 2008; **148(l)** GC/Liz Eddison, **(c)** GAP/Friedrich Strauss, **(br)** PI/GPL/Janet Seaton; **149(l)** PL/GPL/Richard Bloom, **(tr)** GC/Kim Taylor, **(bc)** BC/Jacqui Hurst, **(br)** GC/Nicola Stocken Tomkins; **150** GAP/Friedrich Strauss; **152** GAP/Friedrich Strauss; **154** PL/GPL/Janet Seaton; **156** PL/GPL/Richard Bloom; **158** PL/GPL/Juliette Wade; **160** Red Cover/Johnny Bouchier; **162** PL/Red Cover/Huntley Hedworth; **164** Alamy/Neil Holmes; **166** GC/Nicola Stocken Tomkins; **168** GC/Jacqui Hurst/Artist Maggy Howarth; **170** GC/Liz Eddison; **172** GC/Kim Taylor.

KEY

GC = The Garden Collection; GAP = GAP Photos; GPL = Garden Picture Library; PL = Photolibrary.com.

Eaglemoss Consumer Publications Ltd

Electra House, Electra Way, Crewe, Cheshire, CW1 6WZ

Telephone 01270 270050 Website www.dairydiary.co.uk

First printed January 2010 © Eaglemoss Consumer Publications Ltd

ISBN-13: 978-0-9560894-2-7

123456789

Contents

Spring

Summer

Autumn

Winter

Gardening is for everyone

A garden offers an abundance of pleasure, relaxation, food and a chance to exercise your artistic talents – all without ever having to leave home!

In the British Isles gardening is a very seasonal activity – the spring garden looks very different from the summer one, and autumn and winter are different again. The aim is to have something of colour and interest in the garden for as long as possible. And the best way to do this is to mix and match the various different types of plants – trees, shrubs, perennials, annuals, biennials and bulbs. You can do this in beds and borders and containers of every size and shape.

Combine your planting with a range of 'hard' features – fences, walls, patios, paths, arches and so on – and you can create a garden that is

Space is no object. Even if you don't have a garden, you can grow things on a windowsill, put a few pots by the front (or back) door, or plant a hanging basket. Even if it's no more than a pot of mint or basil in the kitchen, you can always grow something. And if you have a bit of a garden at the back or front of the house, then you have the start of something that can be just a hobby or the beginning of a life-long passion!

The sheer range of beautiful colours, forms, sizes and scents on offer in the plant world is staggering – truly something for everyone.

a pleasure to be in from one end of the year to the other. Think of it in terms of a series of projects – planting a patio container, a rose bed or a hanging basket, laying a path, painting a fence or edging a lawn, growing herbs for the kitchen or strawberries for the summer – and you'll find making a garden much easier.

The ideas shown in this book can be followed exactly, or act as a starting point for your own creativity. Choose your own favourite flowers and other plants and feel free to adapt the plans and the colour schemes to suit yourself. It's your garden – enjoy it to the full!

How to use this book

For the purposes of this book, spring is taken as March, April and May; summer as June, July and August; autumn as September, October and November; and winter as December, January and February.

Remember that the dates of first and last frosts will vary considerably up and down the country, and high and low temperatures will also vary accordingly; likewise high winds and rainfall.

The seasonal chapters show each project at the time of year when it will look at its best (producing most flowers or fruit), not necessarily when it is to be planted. The months highlighted in white (and the planting calendar overleaf) show you when to tackle each project. The shade, partial shade and sun icons – below the calendar – suggest where it can be sited.

Variations in climate. Check the weather forecast for your area and adjust planting times as necessary.

Many plants are available in the garden centre quite early, but availability does not mean they can be planted out immediately. Also, species and varieties of plants have a range of different flowering and fruiting times; some will be over quite quickly, while others may flower for months and months.

Get to know your plants – and try to give them the optimum conditions wherever possible.

When to tackle the projects

Spring

Spring is the season for revelling in the exuberant yellow, purple, mauve and pink hues of early bulbs and blossoms – to the gardener the new shoots, green leaves and first bursts of flower colour are little short of intoxicating.

In spring you are infused with new energy, filled with fresh plans and fired with enthusiasm for the gardening season ahead. Containers start to come into their own in spring – start with a big bowl of grape hyacinths on the patio, then follow up with narcissi, hyacinths and tulips for a brilliant season-long display. Also plan your bedding schemes of annuals and new shrubs and perennials for the border – but keep an eye out for frosty weather. By May your garden will be crammed with colour and interest.

Blue is Beautiful

There's absolutely no limit to the containers you can press into use for great garden displays. Get off to an early start in spring with this brimming trough of grape hyacinths.

JAN	FEB	MAR
APR	MAY	JUN
JUL	AUG	SEPT
OCT	NOV	DEC

Plant the corms in September/October for flowering from February through to April.

Can be completed in one hour.

What you need

Plants

20–30 grape hyacinth (*Muscari armeniacum*) corms. The exact number depends on the size of your container.

Equipment

Shallow galvanized tin or enamel trough or container/pot of your choice with several drainage holes punched in the bottom.

Broken crocks for drainage.

Bulb compost to fill container nearly full.

Trowel.

1 **Buy your grape** hyacinth corms in September or October, looking out for ones that are firm, dry and plump with no signs of mould or damage. If you buy them in closed bags, discard any that are shrivelled, damp, mildewed or damaged.

2 **Line the bottom** of the dry container with crocks for drainage, then fill nearly full with bulb compost.

3 **Sit the corms** on the compost, placing them no more than 2.5cm (1in) apart, twisting slightly to firm them in. Place the container in a sheltered spot outside and leave until the flower spikes start to show (the narrow, leaves will appear first).

4 **Move the container** to a sunny spot to display them to maximum effect. The flowers do best in full sun and provide a welcome burst of colour on a patio or in the corner of a courtyard. Water lightly if the weather is dry or if the leaves show signs of wilting.

Tip

Look out for white varieties of grape hyacinth as an alternative to the usual blue, and plant them in a second container, or mix them together for a most attractive display.

Note

Cut grape hyacinth flower spikes are excellent for miniature indoor flower arrangements.

Aftercare

Remove dead flower spikes as they wither. When all the flowers have gone, leave the container in an out-of-the-way corner until the leaves have died down. The plants probably won't put on enough new leaf growth for the corms to produce a good container flower display again the following year. If you wish, you can plant the corms in the garden in early autumn, setting them 7.5cm (3in) deep and 10cm (4in) apart.

Pretty in Pink

Make a pretty basket of pink hyacinths special by adding hoops of pussy willow twigs with the soft grey catkins just bursting out – a lovely display that should last for several weeks. Enjoy the heavenly scent produced by the hyacinths.

JAN	FEB	MAR
APR	MAY	JUN
JUL	AUG	SEPT
OCT	NOV	DEC

Pussy willow twigs are available in early spring, either in hedgerows or from florists. Pot-grown hyacinths can be found in garden centres from January through to May or even later.

Planting up a basket takes about an hour.

What you need

Plants

Ten to twelve pink Dutch hyacinths just coming into flower.

Six to eight pussy willow twigs each about 45cm (18in) long. (Pussy willows are the male catkins on the twigs of goat willow – *Salix caprea* – and they appear long before the leaves.)

Equipment

Rustic-weave basket.

Hanging-basket liner (plastic, hessian, felt or moulded paper).

Bulb compost to fill.

Several handfuls of moss to tuck around the base of the hyacinths.

Trowel.

1 Place the liner you have chosen in the bottom of the basket, pricking holes through for drainage if needed. Fill the basket two-thirds full with bulb compost.

2 Carefully remove each hyacinth, one at a time, from their pots and plant in the basket, adding more compost and setting each one to the same depth as it was in its pot. Place them as close together as you can, so the heavy flowerheads will support each other, and firm in well.

3 Tuck moss loosely around the base of the hyacinths to cover the soil completely. Water lightly.

4 Wedge the bottom end of a pussy willow twig into the basket weave then bend it over to form a hoop. Tuck the tip of the twig securely into the basket, then repeat with the other twigs all round the basket, overlapping the twigs slightly as you go.

5 Position your basket in a sunny spot for best display. The furry grey catkins will eventually turn bright yellow as they open.

Tips
Take great care not to knock the pussy willow catkins off the twigs as you handle them – they are quite fragile. If the hyacinth stems start bending over, insert thin bamboo canes into the compost and tie the stems to them as discreetly as possible with soft string. Bring under shelter if heavy rain is threatened.

Note
Reuse your rustic basket for a summer display by planting with nasturtiums or begonias.

Aftercare
By its very nature this is a temporary display. When the hyacinth flowers have withered, stop watering and allow the foliage to turn brown. Then remove the bulbs from the basket, clean them carefully and store in a dry, dark place until autumn, when you can plant them out in the garden. Discard the pussy willow twigs when the catkins have flowered.

Spring Flower Medley

The beauty of growing plants in pots is that you can bring very different species together to form interesting associations – as proved by this captivating little group themed around the colour blue.

JAN	FEB	**MAR**
APR	MAY	JUN
JUL	AUG	SEPT
OCT	NOV	DEC

Buy the different plants and pot up in March for flowering in April and May.

Takes about one hour.

What you need

Plants

Three deep blue hyacinths (*Hyacinthus orientalis* 'Delft Blue'), in leaf, flower buds showing.

Five to seven *Iris reticulata* 'Harmony' in leaf.

Ten to twenty grape hyacinths (*Muscari armeniacum*).

Three small pots of *Anemone blanda* 'Violet Star'.

One large pot of trailing variegated ivy (*Hedera helix*).

Equipment

Three blue ceramic pots (or any other containers of your choice).

Two small terracotta pots.

One watering can with a wide mouth.

Enough soil-based potting compost to fill all the containers.

Broken crocks for drainage.

Horticultural grit or gravel (optional).

Trowel.

1 **Water all the** plants thoroughly so the rootballs are moist right through. Line all the containers with a layer of broken crocks for drainage.

2 **Start filling each** container with compost. About halfway up, place the plant in its pot into the container to check for the right level. The top of the rootball should be about 4cm (1½in) below the rim of the container. Add more compost as needed.

3 **Carefully tip each** plant out of its pot, supporting the rootball and compost with your fingers on each side of the plant stems. Place in the container, firming in gently, then top up with more compost around the plant, aiming to keep the top of the compost 4cm (1½in) below the container rim. Firm the plant(s) again, then lift the container and tap it gently against the ground to settle the compost and even it out.

4 **Repeat the planting** procedure for all the containers and plants. Water them all thoroughly using a fine rose on your watering can. If you like, scatter a layer of horticultural grit or gravel on top – this will keep weeds at bay, help to retain moisture and look neat.

5 **Finally, position the** newly planted containers in their allotted spot and wait for them to flower.

Tip
Choose a spot in full sun for the *Anemone blanda* – these will only open fully when the sun is shining right on them.

Note
When choosing your containers, bear in mind overall size and height. The aim is to have a range of sizes from short at the front to tall at the back.

Aftercare
Support the top-heavy hyacinths with discreet bamboo canes and soft string ties if needed.

As with most bulbous plants, when the hyacinths, grape hyacinths and iris have finished flowering, allow the leaves to die back completely before lifting the bulbs/corms/rhizomes and planting in the garden. Alternatively, discard the old plants and replace next year with new.

Playing a Supporting Role

A single giant pot with a very large plant can look a bit stark – surrounding it with smaller containers holding a variety of colourful flowers will soften the overall effect.

JAN	FEB	MAR
APR	MAY	JUN
JUL	AUG	SEPT
OCT	NOV	DEC

Buy a bedding strip of pansies, and several pots of white narcissi in bud in March for flowering in April and May.

Planting one pot like this takes less than an hour, but if you want to surround a large container with many smaller ones, allow an afternoon for the job.

What you need

Plants

Bedding strip of six to eight blue pansy (*Viola*) plantlets.

Six white *Narcissus* 'Petrel' in bud.

Equipment

Terracotta pot.

Soil-based potting compost.

Broken crocks for drainage.

Trowel.

Extra terracotta pots, if required, to surround the planted container.

1 **Line the terracotta** pot with a layer of broken crocks for drainage.

2 **Start filling with** compost, then ascertain the right height for the narcissi by placing them in their pot on the compost – the rootball/bulbs should be about 4cm (1½in) below the rim of the terracotta pot.

3 **Position all the** narcissi, spacing them out as evenly as possible, firm in by twisting each one slightly, then top with more compost.

4 **Plant the pansies** in the same way, positioning them around and in front of the pot. Firm them in, finishing with a final layer of compost. Bump the pot gently to settle the plants and compost, then water thoroughly.

Tip

The beauty of this arrangement is that when the pansies and narcissi have finished flowering, you can replace the whole pot with another display. With the wide range of narcissi and pansy colours available, you can choose any number of variations on this theme – or go for something completely different.

Note

The pansies may well flower a lot longer than the white narcissi. In this case, cut down the narcissi stalks when the flowers have withered and allow the pansies to continue on their own.

Aftercare

Deadhead the pansies regularly to ensure a long and continuing display of flowers. If the narcissi start bending over (in high winds or rain), support with thin bamboo canes and soft string ties.

Ranunculus and Anemones

Here's a pretty spring version of buttercups and daisies – double-flowered deep yellow *Ranunculus* buttercups teamed with daisy-like purple anemones grown in a hollowed-out tree stump.

JAN	FEB	MAR
APR	MAY	JUN
JUL	AUG	SEPT
OCT	NOV	DEC

Plant tubers of *Anemone blanda* in autumn for flowering from early spring to early summer. Plant *Ranunculus* in early spring for flowering in late spring and through to summer – they form clumps, so allow three plants to a pot.

Planting should take an hour or so to complete.

What you need

Plants

Nine pot-grown Persian buttercups (*Ranunculus asiaticusacris*).

Three or four small pots of windflower (*Anemone blanda*).

Equipment

Three pots with drainage holes.

Hollowed–out tree stump, or other wide, shallow container with drainage holes.

Hanging-basket liner (plastic, felt, hessian).

Soil-based potting compost.

Broken crocks for drainage.

Trowel.

1 **Prepare the hollow** tree stump for planting by digging out any loose or rotten wood, excavating a cavity large enough to take compost and several anemone plants.

2 **Plant the anemones** in September. Line the cavity with the liner you have chosen, pricking small holes in the bottom if necessary. Fill with compost. Plant the anemone tubers about 5cm (2in) deep and 10cm (4in) apart. Firm in and top up with more compost if needed.

3 **Plant the buttercups** in early spring. Line the pots with broken crocks for drainage, then half-fill with compost. Plant the buttercups three to a pot, then firm in and top up with more compost. Water well.

4 **Place the buttercups** and the anemone tree trunk in a sunny sheltered site in spring – the anemones in particular need full sun to open completely. Place the taller buttercups behind the low-gowing anemones.

Tips
The buttercups make excellent cut flowers for a vase indoors. Tuck a little florist's moss under and around the anemones in the tree stump for a more natural, woodland look.

Note
Both these plants are frost hardy and should provide spring interest for several years.

Aftercare
Water the containers if the weather is very dry. Deadhead the buttercups to encourage more flowers to develop. The anemones disappear completely in summer, but pop up again very early next spring.

Tulip and Pansy Basket

Elegant apricot yellow tulips, early flowering mixed pansies and dramatic trailing variegated ivy make a stylish combination in this unusual – and delightful – late spring hanging basket.

JAN	FEB	MAR
APR	MAY	JUN
JUL	AUG	SEPT
OCT	NOV	DEC

Plant in early spring for mid to late spring flowering.

Can be completed in about an hour.

What you need

Plants

20 bulbs of *Tulipa batalinii* 'Apricot Jewel' in pots.

Mixed pansies – here there are six different coloured varieties.

Four pots of trailing variegated ivy *(Hedera helix)*.

Equipment

Hanging basket with hook and chain.

Hanging basket liner (plastic, hessian, felt or moulded paper).

Potting compost.

Trowel.

1 **Line your hanging** basket to prevent the compost falling out, then add a layer of compost at the bottom.

2 **Position the four** ivy plants first, setting them at equal distances around the edge of the basket, firming them into the compost at the bottom and feeding the foliage through the holes in the side. Add more compost around and on top of the ivy.

3 **Next position the** tulip bulbs, spacing them as evenly as possible but setting them in at least two distinct layers around the basket, adding more compost and firming in as you go.

4 **Finally put in** the pansies. Tuck these in as close together as possible, pushing the foliage through the side holes and firming the soil all around the rootballs. Finish by planting pansies across the top and centre of the basket covering all the bare compost – but leaving the centre slightly lower than the sides to make watering easier.

5 **Water thoroughly with** a fine rose. Then hang the basket in its final position, making sure that the hanging bracket or eye is secure and can take the considerable weight of the basket.

Tips

To maintain the good appearance of the display and to keep the plants flowering as long as possible, deadhead frequently. This will encourage new flowers to form. Don't allow the pansies to set seed. Regularly remove any dead or discoloured leaves from the ivy.

Note

Leaving at least 2.5-5cm (1-2in) of space above the compost in the basket assists with water retention.

Aftercare

Hanging baskets and window boxes contain a lot of plants for the amount of soil in their container, so feed regularly throughout the growing/flowering season with a liquid fertiliser or with fertiliser spikes inserted into the compost at planting time. Water frequently to ensure the plants don't dry out – especially, if the basket is hanging in a sheltered position where rain can't reach too easily.

Spring Beauty in a Basket

Brighten up the garden in spring with a hanging basket full of colour – position it where it can be seen easily and where it can catch the sun. Avoid a windy area where the basket could swing too much.

JAN	FEB	MAR
APR	MAY	JUN
JUL	AUG	SEPT
OCT	NOV	DEC

Plant in early spring for flowering in March and April.

Planting should take an hour or two.

What you need

Plants

Four to six pots of *Narcissus* 'Hawera' with the leaves just showing.

Four to six pots of pansies (*Viola*).

Three or four pots of grape hyacinths (*Muscari*).

One plant of *Senecio cineraria* 'Silver Dust'.

Equipment

Hanging basket with chains and hook – if you can't find a blue one, buy an ordinary brown one and paint it with a non-toxic proprietary wood paint.

Hanging-basket liner (plastic, felt, hessian or moulded paper).

Potting compost.

Trowel.

1 **Line the basket** with the liner, pricking small holes through if necessary. Half-fill with compost.

2 **Plant the senecio** first, at the back of the basket. Firm in then top up with more compost.

3 **Plant the narcissi** next, spreading them around the centre of the basket and to the sides. Again, firm in and top up with compost. Plant the grape hyacinths in the same way, placing them in front of the narcissi.

4 **Finally, plant the** pansies, setting them at intervals around the front of the basket. Firm in, then top up with compost to within 4cm (1½in) of the rim of the basket. Water thoroughly.

5 **Hang the basket** securely from the branch of a tree, or in any position in the garden that gets a reasonable amount of sun.

Tip
If the narcissi start to droop – or are suffering in the wind – support them with thin canes and soft string.

Notes
When the flowering display is over, and the leaves of the narcissi have turned brown, transplant the pansies and senecio to a sunny spot in the garden – or to a pot. Dry off and clean the bulbs and keep in a dry, dark place until autumn, when they can be potted up again.

Aftercare
Keep the basket well watered. Deadhead the flowers as they wither.

Two-colour Tulip Border

Achieving a glorious spring border display of tulips like this takes a bit of planning but the spectacular results are well worth the time and effort spent.

JAN	FEB	MAR
APR	MAY	JUN
JUL	AUG	SEPT
OCT	NOV	DEC

Aim to plant the tulip bulbs in November or December for flowering in May.

For this quantity of tulips, you may need to set aside two afternoons. Note here that more tulips - white ones - have been planted to face the lawn.

What you need

Plants

You usually get only one flowerhead per bulb, so for this size of display buy at least 50 bulbs of each tulip variety – 'Queen of the Night' (nearly black) and 'Angelique' (pink) are good varieties to choose.

Equipment

Garden fork and spade.

Trowel or bulb planter.

Garden lime (if needed).

1 **Prepare your garden** soil well. To achieve the best results, choose a site in full sun and with well-drained soil. Dig the area over in October, removing stones and weeds and adding soil-based compost as you go. If you don't want to lift the bulbs every year, also add a sprinkling of garden lime, following the manufacturer's instructions.

2 **Plant the bulbs** 15-20cm (6-8in) deep and 10-20cm (4-8in) apart, using a trowel or bulb planter to make holes for each bulb. For an informal effect, try scattering the bulbs at random over the area and planting them where they fall. For a more formal look, set the two colours of tulips in an alternating pattern. Firm each bulb in by twisting slightly, then cover with soil, making sure you don't leave any air pockets which could cause the bulbs to rot.

Notes

Unlike daffodils, tulip bulbs have a tendency to deteriorate if left in the ground, so many gardeners lift them when the foliage has turned yellow and store them in a frost-free place until late autumn/early winter, when they can be planted out again – but not in the same place! Planting the bulbs deep enough and in a very free-draining lime-rich soil means they can be left for a maximum of three years before they must be lifted. By their very nature, tulip beds/borders are temporary.

This border has forget-me-nots and various other herbaceous plants intermingled with the tulips. To get this full effect is a major garden project which will probably take several seasons to complete.

Aftercare

Deadhead flowers as they fade, and pull away foliage as it turns brown – but not before since the green leaves feed the bulb below so that it can produce another flower the following year. Lift the bulbs (if you are going to, see Notes left) when the foliage has withered and dry the bulbs, then store in a frost-free place until November/December.

Crown Imperials and Tulips

Crown imperials are one of the stateliest plants in the herbaceous border – here they are partnered by a winding band of forget-me-nots and double-flowered tulips that echo their fiery red colour.

JAN	FEB	MAR
APR	MAY	JUN
JUL	AUG	SEPT
OCT	NOV	DEC

Plant the crown imperials and tulips in late autumn and the forget-me-nots in spring. They will flower in April.

The time it takes to plant this type of bed depends on its size.

What you need

Plants

Six to ten bulbs of crown imperial (*Fritillaria imperialis*).

At least 12 double early orange-red tulips, such as 'Orange Nassau'.

Several bedding strips of forget-me-nots (*Myosotis* 'Royal Blue' or a similar variety).

Equipment

Garden fork and spade.

Garden compost.

Coarse sand.

Bamboo canes for staking (if necessary).

1 **Choose a sunny** site. Dig the ground where the plants are to grow at least a month before planting. Fork in a dressing of garden compost.

2 **To plant the** crown imperials, dig a hole for each bulb about 20cm (8in) deep. Line the hole with coarse sand and lay a scaly bulb sideways on it. Cover with more sand and then fill the hole with soil. Repeat for all the bulbs, spacing them at least 45cm (18in) apart.

3 **Plant the tulips,** leaving a sufficiently wide band of ground for the forget-me-nots in front of the crown imperials. Plant the tulips about 20cm (8in) deep and about 20cm (8in) apart.

4 **In spring, plant** the forget-me-nots in a wide band between the crown imperials and the tulips. Plant them about 5cm (2in) deep and 20cm (8in) apart. Water the bed well, especially in dry weather.

5 **If necessary, stake** the crown imperials with bamboo canes – they can reach a height of 90cm (3ft). This combination should reach peak flowering in April.

Tip
Crown imperials are available in red, yellow and orange colourways – try planting a mixture in a herbaceous border for a sizzling spring display.

Notes
Forget-me-nots self-seed easily and can invade a garden. The crown imperials can be left undisturbed for three or four years, after which they need to be lifted and divided.

Aftercare
Deadhead the crown imperials and tulips when the flowers have faded.

Sizzling Spring Colour

Set a sunny corner alight in your spring garden with sizzling hot cerise and orange tulips teamed with yellow and orange wallflowers – they'll catch and reflect every last ray of sunshine and warm up the coldest day.

JAN	FEB	MAR
APR	MAY	JUN
JUL	AUG	SEPT
OCT	NOV	DEC

Buy bedding strips of seedling wallflowers and tulip bulbs in October and plant in the bed where they are to grow. They will flower from March to May.

Planting should take about an hour.

What you need

Plants

Ten or more 45-60cm (18-24in) tall lily-flowered orange tulip bulbs and the same number of cerise tulip bulbs, depending on the size of your bed or border.

Bedding strips of yellow and orange wallflowers (*Erysimum [Cheiranthus] cheiri*).

Equipment

Garden fork or spade.

Trowel.

1 **Wallflowers like very** well drained, alkaline soil which isn't too rich, and a sunny site. Dig over the area where they are to be grown a week or two before planting, removing weeds, roots and stones.

2 **Put in the** tulip bulbs first, setting them towards the back of the border – plant them 15-20cm (6-8in) deep and about 10-20cm (4-8in) apart. Twist each bulb slightly in its planting hole to settle them in.

3 **Plant the wallflower** seedlings in front of and around the tulips, setting them to the same depth as they were in their bedding strips, and about 20cm (8in) apart. Mix up the colours to suit your own taste. Firm in the seedlings, then pinch out the top growing tip of each, to encourage bushy growth.

4 **Water the whole** bed gently using a fine rose on your watering can.

Tips

Try to grow wallflowers close to the house if possible – the flowers are fragrant and you can pick up wafts of their sweet scent as you pass by. Various other colours are available.

Notes

Wallflowers are perennial but are usually treated as hardy biennials. They will survive winter and even flower for a couple of years after planting, but they tend to grow straggly and woody, so it's generally best to plant new seedlings every year. Wallflowers are often sold as bare-rooted plants tied in bunches of 12 or so. The tulips should be lifted after their leaves have withered – keep the bulbs in a dry, dark place and replant in autumn.

Aftercare

Water regularly in dry weather. Deadhead the flowers when they have withered.

Bright and Beautiful Border

The rich reds and purples of *Anemone coronaria* make a bold splash of colour in a warm and sheltered spot – they cut quite a dash when teamed with tall red tulips against the backdrop of an old stone wall.

JAN	FEB	MAR
APR	MAY	JUN
JUL	AUG	SEPT
OCT	NOV	DEC

Plant the anemones in September or October for March or April flowering. Add the tulips in November.

Planting should take about an hour.

What you need

Plants

20 tubers of *Anemone coronaria* 'de Caen' strain.

10-12 tulip bulbs – 'Ballerina' is a good red variety.

Equipment

Garden spade and fork.

Trowel.

Bamboo canes.

1 **Prepare the border** well before planting. Anemones need a sunny spot with humus-rich soil. Dig over the site in early autumn, removing stones and weeds. Enrich with humus-rich compost if needed.

2 **Soak the anemone** tubers overnight before planting. Plant 5cm (2in) deep and about 10cm (4in) apart. Water thoroughly.

3 **Since you are** putting in the tulips later than the anemones, mark the sites for the tulips – interspersed among the anemones – with bamboo canes so you don't disturb the anemones.

4 **Plant the tulip** bulbs 15-20cm (6-8in) deep, twisting each one slightly to firm it in and covering with a packing of soil to eliminate air pockets.

Tip
Anemone coronaria makes excellent cut flowers for a vase indoors.

Notes
You can divide mature clumps of *Anemone coronaria* in late summer. Replant immediately. For best display, replace the tulips every year.

Aftercare
Deadhead the anemones to keep them flowering for as long as possible. Also deadhead the tulips, then remove withered foliage.

Pot Herbs for the Kitchen

Fresh herbs give a great lift to many foods – so grow your own in pots sited near the kitchen for ease of picking. And why not choose some colourful, fun containers to plant in?

JAN	FEB	MAR
APR	MAY	JUN
JUL	AUG	SEPT
OCT	NOV	DEC

Sow seeds in March, or buy small herb plants in April or May, pot up at once and start picking leaves as soon as the plants have grown slightly.

The job will take about an hour.

What you need

Plants

Seed packets or small plants of parsley, thyme, marjoram (oregano), sage, mint and rosemary.

Equipment

Six small plastic pots for potting up seedlings bought at the garden centre.

Seed tray, modular cell system or jiffy pots for sowing seeds, if using.

Five containers such as the enamel kettles.

Soil-based potting compost and proprietary seed compost if using.

Broken crocks for drainage.

Trowel.

1 **Fill the seed** tray or modular cell system with seed compost and sow your seeds according to the instructions on the packets, or sow in jiffy pots according to the manufacturer's instructions. Keep on a kitchen windowsill while the seeds germinate, then move them outside when all danger of frost is past.

2 **When the seedlings** are large enough to handle, pot them on into the plastic pots using potting compost and lining with broken crocks for drainage.

3 **Or, line the** plastic pots with broken crocks and fill with potting compost, into which you have mixed some sharp sand (if using). Then plant your garden centre seedlings, place into the containers and set out in an attractive arrangement. In general, allow one herb per container, but if the container is big enough, put several in together – here rosemary, parsley and mint have been put in the central container.

4 **Place the young** herb plants outside only when all danger of frost is past. If you're uncertain, place them outside on sunny days and bring them in at night until the weather warms up enough for them to be left outside permanently.

5 **Pick and use** the leaves regularly. All these herbs can grow quite large and, by the end of summer, may well have outgrown their containers unless you keep them under control.

Notes

Most herbs do best in full sun. They don't require rich soil, but they must not be allowed to get waterlogged, so good drainage is essential. Rosemary, sage, thyme and marjoram are tough, shrubby plants and can be kept going for years if put into the ground or grown in large enough pots. Mint and parsley are herbaceous and will die down in winter, but reappear again in spring.

Aftercare

Regular picking is needed, and watering with care.

Bijou Bee Home

Pollinating bees are a vital part of a garden's ecology – so give them a helping hand by building a box for them to nest in. All you need are a few pieces of wood – such as pine – and some cut bamboo canes.

JAN	FEB	MAR
APR	MAY	JUN
JUL	AUG	SEPT
OCT	NOV	DEC

You can make this bee box at any time of year. Hang it up in spring, which is when the bees start looking for nesting places.

The time it will take depends on your woodworking skills. Allow an afternoon for the job.

What you need

Equipment

Tape measure, pencil, saw, sandpaper, drill, screws, screwdriver, non-toxic clear varnish, paintbrush, protractor.

Seven pieces of sawn untreated 2cm (¾in) thick timber of the following dimensions: two roof pieces, one 15cm x 15cm (6in x 6in), the other 17cm x 15cm (6¾in x 6in); one 20cm x 20cm (8in x 8in) base piece; four 23cm (9in) lengths of 2cm (¾in) square timber for the side posts, one end of each cut at a 3-5° angle (so the posts will lean out slightly).

Screw-ended hook for hanging up the box.

Lengths of bamboo cut to fit inside the box.

1 Saw all seven pieces of timber to the dimensions given on page38. Sand all the cut edges smooth. Draw a 15cm (6in) square centrally on the base piece of timber. Drill a pilot hole in the base oat each corner. The four posts will be screwed on to the inside corners of this square.

2 Screw the roof pieces together, first drilling pilot holes for the screws – butt the shorter piece up under the longer piece.

3 Place each side post (with square end at the top) on an inside corern of the base (they should lean outwards slightly) and mark with a pencil the angle needed at the top for the roof to fit (48-50°)Then screw the four side pieces to the base piece.

4 Screw the roof to the four posts. Again, drill pilot holes for the screws. The peaked roof will allow rain to run down without getting inside the box.

5 Coat the whole box with a non-toxic clear varnish to protect it from the weather.

6 Cut lengths of bamboo to fit inside the box – each piece of bamboo should be cut just behind a node, so that one end is open and one end closed. Wedge the bamboo pieces tightly inside the box, open ends facing outwards. Build up the bamboo pieces from the bottom upwards.

7 Screw the hook into the back of the roof, then hang it up in a warm, sheltered, secluded place in the garden – ideally facing the morning sun.

Tips

An alternative to this bee box could be a simple log with holes drilled in it. Find a piece of timber and drill holes in it – but not all the way through – then hang it on a fence or post in a warm, south-facing position.

Notes

Don't use insecticide sprays anywhere near your bee box. The female bee will lay eggs inside the bamboo; these hatch into larvae and then form cocoons. They stay in cocoons over winter, then hatch into young bees in spring.

In the picture, a sheet of 1mm aluminium has been hammered around the roof and tacked into place for extra protection against the elements.

Aftercare

The bees most likely to use the box are solitary mason bees which nest in holes in wood but do not drill holes themselves, instead making use of whatever ready-made holes they can find. They do not sting. In spring, after the young bees have hatched from their cocoons, take down the box, clean it out and then hang it up again for the next generation to inhabit.

A Box for the Birds

Encourage small songbirds into your garden with a tailor-made nest box – this small-hole version is suitable for blue and great tits, coal tits and tree sparrows.

JAN	FEB	MAR
APR	MAY	JUN
JUL	AUG	SEPT
OCT	NOV	DEC

You can make the box at any time of year, but try to put it into position in January. Birds can start looking for nesting sites pretty early.

Making the box and putting it up should take an afternoon.

What you need

Equipment

Saw, sandpaper, screwdriver, hammer, tape measure, pencil, drill, drill bits including a 28mm wide bit for the entrance hole.

One piece of sawn, untreated timber measuring 1.2m (4ft) long, 15cm (6in) wide and 1.25cm (¾ in) thick.

Two brass hinges and screws.

Water-based wood preservative and brush.

Hook or strong nail for hanging the box.

1 **Mark out all** the pieces on the timber using tape measure and pencil, to the following dimensions:
- Back 30cm x 15cm (12in x 6in).
- Floor 11cm x 15cm (4.5in x 6in).
- Front 18cm x 15cm (7in x 6in).
- Roof 20cm x 15cm (8in x 6in).
- Side panels x 2 (cut for the sloping roof) 20cm (8in) high at the back, 18cm (7in) high at the front, 15cm (6in) at top and bottom.

2 **Cut out the** six sections accurately with a saw.

3 **Sand all rough** edges smooth – any splinters could damage the birds. Drill several small holes in the floor piece for drainage.

4 **Fix one of** the sides to the floor of the box using three nails set at intervals, then nail both of these to the back section – three nails per join are enough.

5 **Turn the box** on to the fixed side and nail the second side on to the back and floor.

6 **Make the entrance** hole for the birds in the front using a drill and 28mm wide drill bit. Position this hole at least 13cm (5in) up from the floor so the baby chicks can't fall out. Sand the edges of the hole smooth.

7 **Turn the box** on its side and nail the front piece to the sides. Everything should fit together tightly without gaps. Screw the brass hinges on to the roof and back pieces.

8 **Drill a hole** in the top of the bird box for attaching to a tree trunk or branch via a hook or nail. Paint the outside of the box with a water-based wood preservative but do not allow the preservative to get inside the box – it will poison the chicks. Also keep the preservative away from the entrance – the adult birds often tap this area with their beaks before entering.

9 **Position the box** in a sheltered site, preferably between north and east to avoid heavy rain and hot afternoon sun. Place it high enough to be out of reach of prowling cats. Don't position it near a bird feeding table – the constant coming and going of other birds will deter the parent birds from using the box.

Tips

Hanging the box about 2m (7ft) above ground should be enough to deter predators. Tilt the box slightly forwards when fixing it in place to aid water run-off.

Aftercare
Don't be tempted to look in the box while baby birds are inside – such disturbance may cause the parents to desert the nest. Just watch comings and goings from a distance. When the chicks have fledged and left the box, take it down, remove old nesting material and clean it thoroughly with scalding hot water – this is enough to kill any parasites. Reapply water-based preservative if needed to prolong the life of the box, then hang it up again.

Mosaic Bird Bath

This delightful mosaic bird bath makes an eyecatching feature in the garden – its rainbow colours shine like jewels and the bright floral pattern complements the surrounding flowers and foliage to perfection.

JAN	FEB	MAR
APR	MAY	JUN
JUL	AUG	SEPT
OCT	NOV	DEC

Make this in spring and put it out straight away so the birds get used to it and start using it regularly.

It should take about an afternoon to complete, but you must allow plenty of time for the adhesive and grout to dry before putting it outside.

What you need

Equipment

A non-flexible, non-porous base container such as a ceramic or tin tray, or a sealed (glazed) terracotta saucer.

Vitreous glass tiles about 25mm (1in) square in a variety of colours, or ceramic tile squares and glass circles from a craft shop.

Proprietary tile adhesive and grout – both available from craft shops. Here, a dark blue grout has been chosen to complement the colourful tile pattern.

Palette knife or small wooden spatula for applying adhesive. Another wooden spatula for scraping off excess adhesive.

1 To make a pattern like this, you need first to lay out your tiles to check you have the right number and variety of colours. This also makes it easier to apply the tiles in the right sequence.

2 Ensure the surface of the base is clean and dry. Using the palette knife or wooden spatula, apply adhesive to the back of the first tile, 'buttering' it on thinly and following the manufacturer's instructions regarding handling and safety. Apply the first tile to the outside of the base. Here, a row of tiles has been set flush with the rim of the base, while the bottom half of the base has been left bare.

3 Continue in this way all round the outside rim of the base, allowing time for the adhesive to set as you work round so the tiles don't slip off. Each tile is then topped with a glass circle to cover the rim of the container. Glue these in place as before.

4 Start on the inner sides, working methodically with your colours. Inside the base container there are two rows of tiles – offset these as you work round.

5 The pattern on the inside base of your container is the most complicated, so leave this until last. Make sure you are happy with your design (lay it all out on a flat surface first), then complete the pattern. Use another wooden spatula to scrape off excess adhesive.

6 Leave the adhesive to dry thoroughly. Mix the grout according to the manufacturer's instructions and apply it to the gaps between the tiles, on both the inside and outside of the container. Srape off any excess with the wooden spatula. Allow plenty of time for the grout to dry before continuing.

7 Buff up the tile surface with a damp cloth. Position it outside on a raised surface (bricks, an old log or an upturned barrel), fill with clean water and wait for the birds to arrive.

Tips
You can make a 'crazy paving' version of this using broken crockery – either in a single colour theme or with many different colours. Another alternative is very small pebbles – but you'll need to find a reasonable number of these of more or less uniform size.

Notes
Always follow the manufacturer's instructions when using adhesives and grouting, check that they are suitable for the materials you are using before buying, and ensure that they will survive outdoor temperatures and weathering.

Aftercare
Bird baths need regular cleaning and topping up with fresh, clean water. Regular emptying and brushing with hot water and washing-up liquid will keep the bath clear of algae and bird droppings. In winter break any ice that forms so the birds can reach the water, and sweep away any snow. Remove leaves that fall on to the water so they don't rot and discolour the mosaic.

Sleeper 'Stepping Stones'

Gravel and wooden railway sleeper 'stepping stones' make an excellent combination for an area where you don't want grass or flowerbeds – such as this Japanese-style passageway. Spot planting and container plants soften the outlines.

JAN	FEB	MAR
APR	MAY	JUN
JUL	AUG	SEPT
OCT	NOV	DEC

This project can be carried out at any time of year.

Depending on the size of the area to be covered, it should take about a day.

1 Ensure the area to be covered is firm and level (if there is a slope, all the gravel will gradually migrate downhill).

2 Spread gravel over the entire area to a depth of about 10cm (4in). Rake it smooth and level.

3 Position the railway sleepers on top of the gravel – here they are about 30cm (12in) apart and offset to give the effect of a winding path. Set them firmly into the gravel, tapping with the mallet to settle them in properly.

4 Now spread more gravel over the whole area, so that it is flush with the top of the sleepers. Brush the gravel off the sleepers with the broom.

What you need

Equipment

Enough gravel to cover the area to a depth of at least 20cm (8in). (This will be a great deal more than you might think!)

Eight to ten untreated railway sleepers (enquire for these from a garden centre, builder's merchant or reclamation yard). These vary in width and thickness, so choose these first before ordering your gravel.

Wheelbarrow, spade, mallet, rake and garden broom.

5 If you wish to plant anything in the gravel, just trowel it away until you reach the soil, then plant as usual. Replace the gravel round the plant – it will assist drainage and keep weeds at bay.

Tips

Avoid buying railway sleepers coated with a wood preservative such as creosote. These are poisonous to plants – and are nowadays banned from garden use. Untreated, new railway sleepers in various sizes are available.

Notes

Sitting the sleepers on top of a bed of gravel makes for good drainage and ensures that the wood will not rot because of contact with wet soil. Railway sleepers are extremely heavy, so handle with care.

Aftercare

Keep the sleepers free from gravel by brushing occasionally. Bear in mind that they may become slippery in wet weather.

Miniature Millstone Fountain

A water feature enhances any garden. This charming self-contained example has a central mini-millstone with a bubble fountain that allows water to trickle over the stone and the smooth surrounding pebbles.

1 **This type of** small water feature consists of a simple pump-and-sump kit. The reservoir sump, pump and bubble fountain are designed and fitted all together. The water sits in the reservoir, the submersible pump pushes the water up through an outlet pipe and fountainhead set in the centre of the millstone and the water drains back into the reservoir – and so on in a continuous cycle.

2 **Choose your site** – level ground is best since it causes the fewest problems. Dig a hole large enough to take the reservoir and insert it carefully, backfilling with soil to ensure it sits firmly in the hole with no gaps around it.

3 **Install the pump** and its cable in the reservoir, fill with water, then fit the cover and millstone, following the

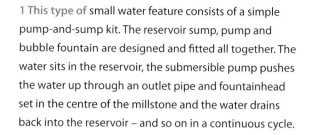

JAN	FEB	MAR
APR	MAY	JUN
JUL	AUG	SEPT
OCT	NOV	DEC

This project can be carried out at any time, but early spring is best because you can plant round it immediately and the water feature will be functioning for the rest of the gardening year. Installing a water feature kit should take a day.

What you need

Equipment

Electricity supply – the bubble fountain is powered by a pump which runs off low-voltage electricity, supplied via a socket sited indoors (in a garage, kitchen etc) and which has an RCD (residual circuit breaker).

Buy the millstone, reservoir (sump), cover (metal grille, grid or strong mesh), pump and fountainhead as an all-in-one kit. The millstone may be made of genuine stone or be of composition stone and fibreglass. Buy a reservoir large enough for its cover to hold both the millstone and the pebbles.

Pebbles to cover the area surrounding the millstone.

Spade (for digging hole to take reservoir sump).

manufacturer's instructions throughout. Fit the outlet pipe and fountainhead in the centre of the millstone.

4 Fill the margins around the millstone with pebbles, sitting them on the metal grille or mesh cover.

5 Run the pump cable to your electric socket and plug it in, following the manufacturer's instructions. You should be able to adjust the water flow by a valve on the outlet pipe of the pond pump so that water bubbles out of the fountainhead, washes over the millstone and pebbles and falls back into the reservoir.

Tip

For cleaning, repair or any rearrangement of any part of the water feature, always remember to unplug the electrical cable before starting work – safety first with anything involving water and electricity is essential.

Notes

The beauty of this type of water feature is that it provides all the interest and pleasure of a pond without the time and effort required to install a pond – and it is child-safe! Remember, though, that there is a cable running from the water feature to the electric socket through the garden; site it safely so people can't trip over it.

Aftercare
The reservoir will need regular topping up, especially after warm or windy weather which increases the rate of water evaporation. Don't let the water level fall so low that the pump is uncovered. Follow the manufacturer's instructions for use of the fountain during the winter months.

Summer

It's summer – and there's everything to play for, with a glorious profusion of growth and colour in the garden. This is also the busiest season, with more than enough to do in the way of planting and maintaining everything in tip-top condition.

Summer is the season when your individual choice and style of garden become important. Are you going in for bedding in a big way, with a riot of colours from plants that bloom their hearts out all summer long? Or is the herbaceous border more your sort of thing, with reliable plants that flower regularly year after year? Perhaps you go for the mixed garden, with small trees and shrubs, perennials, a few annuals for edging – and always a bit of space somewhere to pop in just one more must-have item. Whatever your choice, there is always room for a few well-placed containers, hanging baskets, windowboxes or raised beds with all your favourite flowers.

Rhapsody in Blue

As spring gives way to summer, the range of flowers you can grow outside in containers becomes ever more varied – as this beautiful blue-themed display demonstrates.

JAN	FEB	MAR
APR	**MAY**	JUN
JUL	AUG	SEPT
OCT	NOV	DEC

Plant this combination in May, for flowering throughout the summer.

There are lots of plants to deal with here, so allow a couple of hours for the job.

What you need

Plants

Allow four of each of the following:

Petunia 'Ocean Waves', 'Frenzy' and 'Grand Rapids' (deep purple, mauve and pale blue).

Salvia patens 'Cambridge Blue' and mealy sage (*Salvia farinacea*).

Isotoma axillaris (starry mauve-blue).

Lobelia erinus (white and mid blue varieties).

Equipment

Large white enamel bowl with drainage holes punched in the bottom (or any container of your choice).

Potting compost.

Broken crocks for drainage.

Trowel.

1 **All of the** plants in this combination are annuals – or best treated as such. They will flower all summer long, but won't survive the winter. Choose a sunny position for best results. Water all the plants thoroughly the day before planting.

2 **Line the container** with broken crocks for drainage, then half-fill with compost. Plant the sages first, arranging the plants in a half-circle at the back of the container. Firm in.

3 **Put the** *Isotoma* in next, in front of the sage – again forming a half-circle. Repeat with the petunias next, and finally the lobelias. This is a very 'full' arrangement, so place the plants as close together as you can. The aim, when the plants reach flowering stage, is to give the impression of a profusion of blooms cascading over the sides of the container.

4 **Top up the** container with compost, filling in as much as you can between the plants, firming the soil in with your fingers. The compost should come to about 2.5cm (1in) of the rim. Water using a fine rose on the watering can so you don't dislodge the plants.

Tip
Place this container on a raised support – bricks, an old tree stump or block of wood – so the cascade effect can be seen to best advantage (and so the trailing edges of the plants don't drag along the ground).

Notes
Single colour themes like this can create an air of tranquillity and calm which contrasts well with the riot of different colours that are so often seen in a summer garden. As an alternative, try yellow or pink themes.

Aftercare
With a container as crowded as this, regular watering is essential – keep an eye on it in dry weather and don't allow the plants to wilt. When the plants start flowering, feed with a potassium-rich soluble fertiliser once a week to encourage growth. Deadhead frequently to encourage more flowers.

Handsome Patio Planter

A handsome combination for a site in full sun, this container will provide a long-lasting show throughout the summer. The foliage has as important a role as the flowers here in creating the overall effect.

JAN	FEB	MAR
APR	MAY	JUN
JUL	AUG	SEPT
OCT	NOV	DEC

Plant at the end of May for flowering right through the summer. Planting should take one or two hours.

What you need

Plants

One *Cuphea ignea* (this is a tender evergreen, sometimes called the 'cigar flower').

One *Helichrysum petiolare* 'Variegatum' (the 'liquorice' plant – grown for its cream-variegated leaves).

Three *Lobelia erinus* (choose a dark blue variety).

Equipment

The container shown here is a large antique terracotta pot. Modern terracotta, plastic or ceramic containers are all suitable as long as they have drainage holes in the bottom.

Soil-based potting compost.

Broken crocks for drainage.

Trowel.

1 Both the *Cuphea* and the *Helichrysum* are shrubby, but both are tender – as is the lobelia. Don't put this combination outside until all danger of frost is past. All the plants here require full sun.

2 If you are using a large terracotta or ceramic pot, place it in its permanent position before planting, since it will be too heavy to move once full.

3 Line the container with broken crocks for drainage, then half-fill with compost. Plant the *Cuphea* first, placing it at the back of the container. Firm in, add more compost, then plant the *Helichrysum* to one side.

4 Plant the lobelias in front and to one side, firm in all the different plants, then top up with compost to within 4cm (1½in) of the rim. Water thoroughly.

Tip
Both the lobelia and the *Helichrysum* have a slightly trailing, 'wandering' habit of growth – let them grow as they like, winding in and out of the sturdy, shrubby stems of the *Cuphea*.

Notes
Cuphea ignea is known as the 'cigar flower' because of its long, cigar-shaped red flowers. The flowers also have white-rimmed dark tips that resemble smouldering ash. Although its leaves are evergreen, it is not frost-hardy.

Aftercare
Keep the container well watered, particularly in dry weather – the lobelia's flowers will suffer if it is allowed to dry out. Remove any flowers that appear on the *Helichrysum* – its foliage is its main glory.

A Barrow of Blooms

Here's a novel idea – a fully portable container which can be wheeled to whatever part of the garden needs a 'lift'. Massed pink pelargoniums bloom in riotous profusion in their highly unusual container.

JAN	FEB	MAR
APR	MAY	JUN
JUL	AUG	SEPT
OCT	NOV	DEC

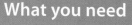

Plant in late spring or early summer. If you deadhead the pelargoniums regularly, they should bloom for months. Allow an afternoon for the planting.

What you need

Plants

Ten or more container-grown pelargoniums.

Equipment

Wheelbarrow (or other container).

Several bags of soil-based potting compost.

Broken crocks, or polythene sheeting for drainage.

Trowel.

1 **Although a wheelbarrow** is an unusual container, treat it like any other. Ensure there are plenty of drainage holes in the bottom of the barrow, then line with broken crocks, or with polythene sheeting into which lots of small holes have been pricked.

2 **Fill the barrow** three-quarters full with compost. Arrange all the pots of pelargoniums on it, moving them around to space them out evenly and give each plant as much room as possible.

3 **Dig a hole** in the compost for each plant, using the trowel, then plant each one in position, firming in as you go. Top up the compost to within 5-7.5cm (2-3in) of the top of the barrow – as they grow, the flowers and foliage will hide most of the barrow. Water thoroughly.

4 **Wheel the planted-up** barrow to its chosen site. Pelargoniums need full sun to produce such a mass of blooms over a long flowering season.

Tip
Using polythene sheeting rather than broken crocks to line the barrow will reduce the overall weight considerably – not a bad thing if the wheelbarrow is fairly old.

Note
The pelargoniums won't survive outdoors in winter. Bring them into a sheltered place – or discard them when they have finished flowering and buy fresh the following spring.

Aftercare
Water regularly – putting so many plants in one container will tend to make it dry out pretty quickly. Deadhead continually to keep the display looking fresh; also remove any brown or withered leaves. Include a liquid feed with your watering once every ten to fourteen days.

Centre Stage Chimenea

An ivy-hatted chimenea takes centre-stage here, surrounded by a cluster of charming smaller pots with pink-themed planting – all meticulously maintained for maximum impact on a decking patio.

JAN	FEB	MAR
APR	MAY	JUN
JUL	AUG	SEPT
OCT	NOV	DEC

Plant in late spring or early summer. With good maintenance, the pots should flower all summer.

There are seven pots here (including one for the ivy at the top of the chimenea); they are very fully planted, so set aside a day to complete the display.

What you need

Plants

Trailing variegated ivy, lilies, pelargoniums, pinks, petunias, lobelias and fuchsias.

Equipment

Chimenea.

Terracotta, plastic or ceramic pots in various sizes – some shallow.

Soil-based potting compost.

Broken crocks for drainage.

Trowel.

1 Place the chimenea in its permanent position. Pot up the ivy in a container lined with broken crocks and filled with compost. Sit the ivy on top of the chimenea – it will soon send out a trailing cascade of variegated foliage.

2 Line all the other containers with broken crocks for drainage, then fill with compost and plant to suit your own taste. Here most of the plant varieties have been given one pot each: petunias, pelargoniums, pinks and so on. The pot on the extreme left has several different items – including a pelargonium, trailing lobelia and a trailing fuchsia.

3 Position all the containers in a semi-circle around the chimenea then water everything thoroughly.

Tip

For extra display on a temporary basis, pop a small pot of a low-growing or trailing plant into the chimenea opening – *Fuchsia* 'Tom Thumb' would fit in well here.

Notes

As the flowers in each container finish blooming, replace with newly planted pots to keep the display going (the ivy will carry on right through winter). Try different colour themes – blue or yellow or all white.

Aftercare

To keep the display looking this good, deadhead meticulously every day. Feed with a liquid fertiliser every ten days or so to encourage flower growth. Also remove any withered, brown or yellowing leaves. And keep a watch for slugs, snails and caterpillars – remove any you see.

Winning Windowboxes

A matching pair of windowboxes livens up this little wooden summerhouse, providing a colourful cottage-garden style display in an ever-popular combination of pink and blue.

JAN	FEB	MAR
APR	**MAY**	JUN
JUL	AUG	SEPT
OCT	NOV	DEC

Plant at the end of May for flowering throughout the summer.
Planting should take about an hour.

What you need

Plants

Four pink snapdragons (*Antirrhinum majus* varieties).

Four dark blue lobelias (*Lobelia erinus* varieties).

Two double-flowered pink petunias (*Petunia hybrida* varieties).

Equipment

Pair of windowboxes with drainage holes at the bottom.

Soil-based potting compost.

Broken crocks for drainage.

Trowel.

1 **Ensure the windowboxes** are clean and dry. If they are attached to a shed or summerhouse, as here, make sure they have not been coated with a toxic wood preservative of any kind.

2 **Line the boxes** with broken crocks for drainage. Half-fill with compost. Plant the snapdragons first, placing them at the back of each box – two to a box. Firm in.

3 **Next plant the** lobelias, one at each end of both boxes. Place the petunias centrally, one in the front of each box, and firm in. Top up both boxes with more compost, then water thoroughly.

4 **These boxes are** placed under the overhanging eaves of the summerhouse roof – which means they will not benefit from natural rainfall. It is therefore vital, if you want a good-looking, long-lasting display, that you water the boxes regularly and often. It will take only one really hot summer day for the flowers to wilt. Use a fine rose on your watering can so the flower petals don't get bruised or waterlogged. Include a soluble feed in your watering regime every ten days or so.

Tips
Annual flowering plants like these bloom very profusely throughout the summer and, after a couple of months, may have exhausted themselves. Once the display is past its best and there don't appear to be many more flower buds forming, discard the plants, clean out the boxes and replant. Try a combination of later summer flowers, such as pink penstemons and pelargoniums, perhaps set off by some grey-foliaged helichrysum.

Note
These plants do best in full sun, so avoid shady sites or those overshadowed by large trees.

Aftercare
Deadhead the flowers regularly to ensure a continuous succession of blooms. Watch for slugs, snails and caterpillars and remove any that you see (the petunias, with their soft, broad leaves, are particularly vulnerable to slug attack).

Fabulous Fern

Here's a show that's strictly for the summer months – a magnificent bird's-nest fern lighting up a shady corner with its huge, wavy-edged, apple-green fronds. Warm, moist conditions in shade are a must – plus indoor shelter for the rest of the year.

JAN	FEB	MAR
APR	MAY	**JUN**
JUL	AUG	SEPT
OCT	NOV	DEC

Grow the fern as an indoor plant until summer temperatures outdoors are warm enough – 16°C (60°F) at the very least. Bring indoors again at the end of summer to a heated greenhouse, conservatory or living room.

Planting the fern should take about a hour or so – it's quite big so will take some handling.

What you need

Plants

A specimen-sized bird's-nest fern (*Asplenium nidus*).

Equipment

Large terracotta, ceramic or plastic container with drainage holes.

Humus-rich compost with added grit or sharp sand for drainage.

Broken crocks for drainage.

Trowel.

1 **Line the container** with broken crocks for drainage. Half-fill with the compost. Check the level of the compost by placing the fern, in its original pot, inside the container – it should be planted at the same level as it was before. Adjust the level of compost as necessary.

2 **Plant the fern** into the compost, firming in well. Top up the compost to within 5cm (2in) of the rim of the pot. Water thoroughly.

3 **Bring the fern** outside when the weather is warm and position in a shady, sheltered spot. Keep it moist at all times and feed weekly with a liquid fertiliser during the growing season.

Tip

If the care, attention and exacting conditions required by bird's-nest fern seem a little daunting, then try its smaller relative, the hart's-tongue fern (*Asplenium scolopendrium*, also known as *Phyllitis scolopendrium* or *Scolopendrium vulgare*). This fern is frost hardy and reaches about 30cm (12in) tall, with a spread of 45cm (18in). It does well in damp, shady places and likes well-drained, alkaline soil. The variety 'Marginatum' has most attractive frilly edged fronds.

Note

If conditions are right, bird's-nest fern can produce fronds over 90cm (3ft) long and 20cm (8in) wide with their trademark thick black midrib. Bear this size in mind for when you need to move the plant around and when it comes to repotting into a larger container.

Aftercare

Remove old or damaged fronds as they appear. Keep warm, moist and humid at all times, though you can lessen watering during the winter.

Fine Foliage Colour

Unusual foliage colour and fine form combine in this tall columnar white container to provide a stunningly elegant display – complemented by surrounding planting that carries on the foliage theme.

JAN	FEB	MAR
APR	MAY	JUN
JUL	AUG	SEPT
OCT	NOV	DEC

Plant in spring for a display that will carry on through summer and into autumn. Allow one or two hours for planting.

What you need

Plants

Two cabbage palms (*Cordyline australis* 'Purpurea').

Coral flower (*Heuchera* 'Palace Purple', 'Obsidian' or 'Licorice').

Three *Bacopa* 'Snowflake'.

Equipment

Tall columnar container with drainage holes at the bottom.

Plastic, terracotta or ceramic pot to fit inside the columnar container.

Wooden battens or bricks to stand inside the container.

Soil-based potting compost.

Broken crocks for drainage.

Trowel.

Four decorative rods (optional).

1 **With a tall** container like this it is unnecessary – and expensive – to fill it all with compost. Place wooden battens or a pile of bricks inside to form a platform for a smaller pot that will fit just inside the container.

2 **Line the inside** pot with broken crocks for drainage, then half-fill with compost. Plant the cordylines first, placing them towards the back of the pot and slightly to each side. Firm in.

3 **Position the heuchera** next, centrally between the cordylines. Finally, plant the three bacopa plants, one right in front of the heuchera and one to each side. Firm in, top up with compost and water thoroughly.

4 **Place the planted** pot inside the columnar container, sitting it on the platform of wood or bricks so that its rim comes just below the rim of the container.

5 **Here, four slender** silver rods have been placed behind the heuchera and between the cordylines to add an extra decorative element.

Tip
A white, cream or otherwise pale background shows off the dark foliage of the cordyline and heuchera to best advantage – and will give some intriguing shadow-shapes in bright sunlight.

Notes
The beauty of this arrangement comes from the contrasting colour and form of the foliage – the spiky deep purple sprays of the cordyline and the more rounded, but matching-coloured leaves of the heuchera being set off to perfection by the small mid green leaves and tiny white flowers of the bacopa. Elegant leaf form is echoed by the surrounding fern fronds, broad hosta and cut-leaved maple.

Aftercare
These plants will thrive in light shade as long as they are kept well watered. The heuchera, which bears long-stemmed bell-like pink flowers, is hardy and will survive winter, but the cordyline may need some protection from frost. The bacopa is evergreen and will send out long trailing stems with white flowers well into autumn.

Bay, Thyme and Lavender

Three strongly aromatic plants combine here to make an enticingly scented corner. A standard bay in a large ceramic pot is circled by a medley of low-growing thymes, with lavender surrounding the base.

JAN	FEB	MAR
APR	MAY	JUN
JUL	AUG	SEPT
OCT	NOV	DEC

Plant in spring. All of these plants have a year-long presence – bay and thyme are evergreen, while lavender, which flowers in summer, retains its grey leaves throughout winter.

Allow a couple of hours to complete this container and the surrounding bed.

What you need

Plants

One bay tree (*Laurus nobilis*), trained to standard shape and clipped to a ball.

Eight thymes (*Thymus serpyllum* and *Thymus citriodorus* varieties – here golden leaved, variegated and grey-leaved forms as well as the more usual dark green).

Eight lavenders (*Lavandula* variety, such as 'Munstead').

Equipment

Large ceramic container (or any other pot large enough to take the bay tree).

Soil-based potting compost with added grit or sharp sand for drainage.

Broken crocks for drainage.

Trowel.

1 **Position your pot** where it is to stand – it will be too heavy to move once planted. Here the pot is surrounded by a narrow bed of lavender which will need about 45cm (18in) of planting space all around the pot.

2 **Line the container** with broken crocks for drainage, then half-fill with compost. Check the level of the bay's rootball by placing it in its original pot on the compost. Adjust the level as necessary to get the rootball to the same depth it was in before, then plant the bay, placing it centrally in the pot. Firm in.

3 **Top up the** container with more compost – the thymes will have much shallower rootballs than the bay. Plant the thymes in a circle around the bay, firm in, then top up again with more compost to within 2.5cm (1in) of the rim. Water thoroughly.

4 **Work some of** the compost/grit mix into the soil around the pot, then plant the lavenders all round. Water thoroughly.

Tips

If you wish, choose a dry, sunny day and cut some of the lavender flowers when they are at their peak. Leave them to dry in bunches, then use them in a vase or a potpourri, or make little sachets and stuff them with the lavender flowerheads – place in linen drawers or hang in clothes cupboards to keep the clothes smelling fresh and sweet.

Note

Both the bay and the thymes are culinary herbs, so use them freely in your cooking.

Aftercare

All these plants do best in full sun and need light, well-drained soil. Keep the bay in shape by trimming any straggly shoots in summer; remove any frost-damaged leaves/shoots in spring. Remove faded lavender flowers in autumn, then prune in April – but do not cut into old wood. Clip the thyme, removing dead flowerheads and straggly shoots in spring.

Glorious Grasses

A number of similar plants brought together in an interesting grouping can have considerable impact – as this collection of container-grown ornamental grasses and bamboos demonstrates.

JAN	FEB	MAR
APR	MAY	JUN
JUL	AUG	SEPT
OCT	NOV	DEC

Plant in spring – some of the grasses and bamboos are evergreen and contribute to the garden display right through the year.

There are at least 10 containers here so planting may take a day – you could carry out over several seasons.

What you need

Plants

A selection of ornamental grasses and bamboos – including blue-leaved and golden-leaved forms as well as green. Look for bamboos (*Arundinaria*), creeping soft grass (*Holcus*), feather grass (*Stipa*), fescues (*Festuca*, especially the blue ones), *Milium*, sedges (*Carex*) and woodrush (*Luzula*).

Equipment

Terracotta, ceramic or plastic containers of various types and sizes with drainage holes at the bottom – almost anything will do.

Soil-based potting compost.

Broken crocks for drainage.

Gravel for the pots to stand on (optional).

Ornamental terracotta or stone balls or other forms (optional).

Trowel.

1 Choose where your collection of bamboos and grasses is to stand. Hard standing such as paving or gravel is a good idea since it sets off the feathery, spiky foliage so well. Equally, a fairly plain background looks good – here there is a trellis fence behind and a bright blue painted shed on the right.

2 Line each of the containers with broken crocks – good drainage is essential for most grasses. Half-fill with compost, check that the level is correct, then plant each grass or bamboo, firming in well, topping up with more compost and watering thoroughly as each is finished.

3 Group the finished containers in an attractive arrangement in full sun or light shade, aiming for varying heights and levels. The bamboos will be the tallest. All the grasses will produce long-lasting flowers, often on long arching stems, throughout the summer. Some of these look like the heads of wheat or oats and are most attractive.

Notes

There are some weird and wonderful botanical names around in the world of bamboos and grasses – so go first for what you like the look of in the garden centre and worry about the botanical details afterwards. Avoid pampas grass *(Cortaderia)*, which grows far too big for containers.

Aftercare

Keep the bamboos and grasses well watered in dry weather. Deadhead the flower stalks when they have withered. Holcus varieties have a tendency to self-seed everywhere, so remove the flowerheads before they turn to seed. Check the plant labels for eventual height and spread, and choose a container of suitable size – or be prepared to repot on a regular basis as the plants grow. Those that die down in autumn will reappear with fresh new growth in spring.

Yucca – a Spiky Specimen

In this modern, beautifully designed courtyard, a grey-leaved yucca has pride of place – it is complemented by a simple planting of pansies and lavender that echo the purple colour scheme of the walls.

JAN	FEB	MAR
APR	MAY	JUN
JUL	AUG	SEPT
OCT	NOV	DEC

You will probably buy the yucca as a sizable specimen plant in summer; it can be repotted immediately and placed where it is to remain, along with its pansy and lavender partners.

Handling a plant of this size takes some doing, so allow a day for it.

What you need

Plants

One beaked yucca (*Yucca rostrata*).

Ten to twelve purple or mauve pansies (*Viola* varieties).

Eight to ten lavenders (such as *Lavandula* 'Hidcote' – a low-growing, deep purple variety).

Equipment

Large terracotta, ceramic or plastic container.

Soil-based potting compost with lots of added gravel or sharp sand.

Broken crocks for drainage.

Trowel.

Heavy-duty gardening gloves.

1 *Yucca rostrata,* a desert plant coming originally from Texas and New Mexico, is one of the hardiest of the yuccas. Its trunk can reach 33m (10ft) or more in height. It likes full sun and poor soil conditions. Away from its desert home, it may need shelter in winter – so choose its site with care.

2 **This yucca has** been placed in the centre of a paved courtyard surrounded by purple walls. Enough room has been left unpaved around the pot so the lavenders have somewhere to grow. Plant the container in situ – it will be too heavy to move once the yucca is in it.

3 **Line the container** with broken crocks for drainage, half-fill with compost, check the yucca will be sitting in the container at the right level, then plant it carefully, firming in well and topping up with more compost. Note: depending on the size of the yucca, you may need more than one person to lift it into place.

4 **Plant the pansies** in a circle around the base of the yucca, firm in, then top up with compost almost to the rim. Water very sparingly – the pansies will need water but the yucca needs almost none.

5 **Work some of** the compost mixture into the soil around the container, then plant the lavenders in a circle around the base of the container and water well.

Tip
An unusual variety of lavender that would look equally good here is *Lavandula stoechas* – which has deep purple flowerheads with large mauve bracts at the tip.

Note
Like all yuccas, this one has very spiky leaves ending in a sharp spine. Handle with care – use heavy-duty gardening gloves.

The planter in the photograph is metal and custom-made to suit the rest of the design.

Aftercare
Deadhead the pansies regularly to encourage more flowers to form. Deadhead the lavender in autumn. The yucca may produce creamy white flowers in summer; remove spent flowers as they fade.

Bountiful Basket

Bursting out all over in a profusion of blooms, this huge blue and yellow themed hanging basket contains no fewer than ten different kinds of plant – they come into flower at different times, so providing a long-lasting display.

JAN	FEB	MAR
APR	MAY	JUN
JUL	AUG	SEPT
OCT	NOV	DEC

Plant in spring for flowering throughout the summer.

There are a lot of plants here, so allow an afternoon for the job.

What you need

Plants

Buy all the plants needed for this basket as small container-grown plantlets.

Three plants are included for their foliage: *Helichrysum petiolare*; creeping Jenny (*Lysimachia nummularia*); and Swedish ivy (*Plectranthus coleoides* 'Variegatus').

Seven are chosen for their flowers: purple heliotrope 'Marine'; petunia; trailing verbena; lobelia; nemesia; French marigold; tradescantia. Note: in the picture, not all plants are in flower.

Equipment

Large hanging basket with chains and hook.

Hanging basket liner (plastic, hessian, felt or moulded paper).

Potting compost.

Trowel.

Slow-release fertiliser spike.

1 **Water all the** plants thoroughly the day before you plan to plant them.

2 **Insert the liner** into the basket – prick small drainage holes through if necessary.

3 **Planting such a** large and varied basket requires a careful building up of layers of plants. Spread a sheet of newspaper or plastic on the ground, then take all your plants out of their original little pots and arrange them in size order on the sheet. Each should be placed in the basket according to the size of its rootball – bigger ones deeper in, smaller ones nearer the top.

4 **Put a layer** of compost into the bottom of the basket. Start planting, spacing the different plants around the basket, firming in, then topping up with more compost. Plant another layer and repeat the procedure. Note that the three foliage plants – the helichrysum, creeping Jenny and Swedish ivy – are all placed at the front so they can trail downwards, while the double-flowered petunia is placed centrally. Deep blue lobelias have been positioned all round the edges.

5 **When the planting** is complete, top up the compost to within 2.5cm (1in) of the top of the basket and insert a slow-release fertiliser spike. Hang it up in its designated position, making sure the hook and fixings are strong enough to take the considerable weight. Water thoroughly.

Tip
Invest in a long-handled, pump-action watering can to make watering your hanging basket easier – and to save you taking it down every day or climbing up a ladder to reach it.

Note
Many, but not all, of these plants are annuals and will not survive the winter. However, even those that are hardy and evergreen, such as the Swedish ivy, will be exhausted by the end of summer – so it's best to discard the whole lot when flowering stops and plant anew in spring.

Aftercare
Water regularly – at least once a day in hot weather. Deadhead withered and faded blooms to prolong flowering and remove any damaged or discoloured foliage.

Foliage Fountain

A bold and impressive array of plants spills out of this eye-catching terracotta hanger like a fountain in full flow – the striking purple, pink and blue colour scheme is not for the faint-hearted!

JAN	FEB	MAR
APR	MAY	JUN
JUL	AUG	SEPT
OCT	NOV	DEC

Plant in late spring or early summer for a display that will last throughout summer. Planting will take an hour or so.

What you need

Plants

Large black Mondo grass (*Ophiopogon planiscapus* 'Nigrescens').

Sedge (*Carex hachijoensis* 'Evergold').

Coral flower (*Heuchera* 'Palace Purple' or 'Licorice').

Morning glory (*Ipomoea tricolor* 'Heavenly Blue').

Two deep pink busy Lizzies (*Impatiens*).

Fairy fan flower (*Scaevola aemula* 'Blue Wonder').

Equipment

Large conical terracotta hanging container (or any other container of your choice), with hanging rods and hook and drainage holes in the bottom.

Broken crocks for drainage.

Potting compost with added sharp sand or grit.

Trowel.

1 **Water all plants** thoroughly the day before planting. If your pot is cone-shaped like the one shown here, prop it up securely while you plant it.

2 **Line the bottom** of the cone with broken crocks for drainage. Fill three-quarters full with the compost mixture.

3 **Plant the black** Mondo grass first, placing it at the back. Firm in well. Place the busy Lizzies next, one each side of the black Mondo grass. Firm in.

4 **Adjust the level** of compost as needed, then plant the coral flower directly in front of the black Mondo grass.

5 **Now deal with** the front planting. Adjust the level of the compost again as necessary. Position the fairy fan flower to the left, the sedge in the centre and the morning glory to the right. Firm in, then top up with more compost to within 2.5cm (1in) of the rim of the container. Insert a slow-release fertiliser spike.

6 **Hang the container** securely in its permanent position, in full sun or light shade. Ensure all hooks and fixings are strong enough to take the full weight of the pot and its plants. Water thoroughly.

Tip
A hanging container like this must have good drainage holes. If the pot you have chosen hasn't got any, use an electric drill to make some in the bottom.

Notes
The fairy fan flower (*Scaevola*), flowering on the extreme left here, is a fairly new plant to become available in garden centres. It hails from Australia and is tender. The morning glory shown here on the right will come in to flower in late summer, bearing deep blue blooms that each last only one day, but are followed by more all the time.

Aftercare
Water well, especially in hot weather. Deadhead the flowers as they fade.

Perfect Pelargoniums

Sometimes sheer simplicity is best. Though many hanging baskets contain a huge variety of different flowers, they don't have to. This lovely pink pelargonium needs no partners to help it create a summer-long display to delight the eye.

JAN	FEB	MAR
APR	**MAY**	JUN
JUL	AUG	SEPT
OCT	NOV	DEC

Plant in late spring for flowering throughout the summer.

Planting should take about half an hour.

What you need

Plants

Two or three deep pink, double-flowered ivy-leaved pelargoniums.

Equipment

Terracotta hanging container with chains and hook and at least one drainage hole in the bottom.

Potting compost.

Broken crocks for drainage.

Trowel.

1 **Line the container** with broken crocks for drainage. Half-fill with compost.

2 **Plant the pelargoniums** into the compost, firm in well, then top up the container with more compost to within 4cm (1½in) of the rim. Water well.

3 **Hang the container** in full sun, preferably in a place where it is sheltered from strong winds.

Tips

Ivy-leaved pelargoniums come in a range of colours – white, pale pink, salmon-pink, deep pink, mauve and magenta. Keep an eye on the weather with your hanging baskets. In wet summers, the pelargoniums will put on leaf growth at the expense of flowers. Place them where they can receive as much sun as possible.

Notes

Bring the container indoors to give the pelargoniums a winter rest. Reduce watering and stop feeding until spring. Then repot in new soil and put outside again when all danger of frost is past.

Aftercare

Keep watered in dry weather, but don't allow the compost to become waterlogged. Deadhead the flowers very regularly to encourage more to appear – with pelargoniums this is crucial to the success of the plant. Also remove any brown leaves. Feed occasionally with a high-potash liquid feed.

Roses all the Way

The rose is the favourite flower of many people – and no wonder, with its beautiful form, variety of colour and heavenly scent. Grown en masse in a bed or border they are a glorious sight to behold.

JAN	FEB	MAR
APR	MAY	JUN
JUL	AUG	SEPT
OCT	NOV	DEC

Plant container grown roses in spring or autumn for flowering throughout the summer. The borders shown here are well established and have taken a couple of years to reach this state of perfection.

For time required see notes.

What you need

Plants

Buy as many rose bushes as you require to fill the space you have in mind. Here, the colour choice has been restricted to pale pink, deep pink and magenta, but you can splash out with every shade of cream, orange, yellow and deep red and an almost infinite variety of pinks. Look for repeat-flowering shrub roses, or low-growing patio roses which are disease-resistant.

Equipment

Fork and spade.

Well-rotted garden manure.

Soil-based compost.

Proprietary rose fertiliser or liquid feed.

1 **Roses are greedy.** In return for blooming their hearts out all summer long they demand deep, humus-rich, well-manured soil, full sun, plenty of water and a regular feeding programme.

2 **Dig over the** rose bed or border several weeks before planting, removing weeds, roots and stones and incorporating well-rotted manure. Water all the roses thoroughly the day before planting.

3 **Plan your colour** scheme. For each rose bush, dig a hole deep enough to take the rootball comfortably – check by placing the plant in its container into the hole. The rose graft (the lumpy area at the base of the stem) should be just above ground level when planted. Line the hole with compost.

4 **Remove the rose** from its container, taking care not to damage the roots. Plant the bush, firming it in thoroughly, then fill the hole with more compost, firm again by treading with your foot, then water thoroughly. Repeat for all the rose bushes.

Tip

Follow your nose. Many modern roses, while having superior disease-resistance and an exceptionally free-flowering habit, have no scent – which is a pity. If you can, go for varieties that have all three qualities.

Notes

Here both sides of a winding gravel path have been charmingly edged with rose bushes – with some lady's mantle (*Alchemilla mollis*) and verbena tucked in between. It's an excellent way of growing lots of roses – the peak display will usually come in June, but you can well have some roses still in bloom in September, especially if you follow the right feeding, deadheading and pruning procedures.

Planting one rose bush in good, well-prepared soil, will take about half an hour – digging the hole, lining with compost or manure, setting the bush in, filling in, firming and treading then watering; planting a whole border, from scratch, will take a long weekend at least. It all depends on how many bushes you have room for, and intend to plant in one go and on the state of the bed in the first place. If the garden soil is heavy clay, it's a devil of a job to dig a hole deep enough for each bush; on light loam it's a doddle!

Aftercare

Follow the instructions on the label for pruning – this varies depending on the type and variety of rose you have chosen. To keep the bushes looking good, deadhead regularly – every day during peak flowering season. Treat as required with proprietary sprays if aphids, black spot or mildew appear. Feed throughout the flowering season, following the manufacturer's instructions on the label.

Circle of Delights

A neatly outlined circular bed of pink, white and blue flowers surrounding a figurine water feature makes a charming summer display in a sunny corner of the garden.

JAN	FEB	MAR
APR	MAY	JUN
JUL	AUG	SEPT
OCT	NOV	DEC

Plant in late spring or early summer for a mid to late summer display.

Allow a day to dig the bed and plant it. Note: the water feature shown here is a custom-built item.

What you need

Plants

Four to six grey-leaved marguerites (*Argyranthemum foeniculaceum*).

Four to six pale pink pelargoniums.

Four to six variegated, scented-leaf pelargoniums.

Mixed white, pink and cerise petunias.

Pink busy Lizzies (*Impatiens*).

Two to four blue *Isotoma axillaris*.

Equipment

Fork, spade and trowel.

String and canes.

General-purpose compost.

1 **Assuming the water** feature is in place, prepare the bed for planting. Outline the circular area using string and canes, then cut it to shape using a sharp spade to remove 30cm (12in) squares of turf and following the string outline closely to ensure a neat edge.

2 **Dig the area** thoroughly several weeks before planting, removing weeds, roots and stones. Incorporate a general-purpose compost as you dig.

3 **Plant the marguerites** and variegated pelargoniums first. Dig a hole for each plant large enough to take the rootball comfortably, spread more compost in the hole, insert the plant, firm in then top up with more compost. Repeat for each plant, alternating the marguerites and pelargoniums in a circle around the water feature. Set the plants 30-45cm (12-18in) apart.

4 **Next comes a** ring of pale pink pelargoniums, planted in the same way in front of the circle of marguerites and set about 30cm (12in) apart. Intersperse the isotomas among the pelargoniums.

5 **Finally, plant the** front ring of petunias and busy Lizzies in the same way, setting them about 20-25cm (8-10in) apart.

6 **Water the whole** bed thoroughly using a fine rose on your watering can.

Tip
Pinch out the stem tips of the marguerites to keep the plants bushy and more compact.

Notes
These plants are not hardy, so clear out the bed in autumn, dig the soil over and replant anew the following summer.

Aftercare
Keep the bed well watered in dry weather and deadhead all the flowers frequently to encourage the production of more.

Courtyard Combination

Planting 'pockets' in a paved area are always eye-catching, the paving providing the plants with a perfect backdrop. Here the effect has been enhanced with a few terracotta pots which offer variety and contrast.

JAN	FEB	MAR
APR	MAY	JUN
JUL	AUG	SEPT
OCT	NOV	DEC

Plant in spring for flowering throughout the summer.

Planting the pots should take no more than an hour; planting the 'pocket' may take an afternoon.

What you need

Plants

Two or three blue *Iris sibirica*; three or four pink *Verbascum*; one or two white rock-cress (*Arabis albida*); one *Convolvulus cneorum* shrub; two or three whitish-mauve African daisies (*Osteospermum jucundum* [*Dimorphotheca jucunda*] variety).

Equipment

Three or more terracotta (or plastic or ceramic) pots with drainage holes.

Broken crocks for drainage.

Garden compost and potting compost.

Garden spade, fork and trowel.

Pebbles of varying sizes for decoration.

1 **Plant the 'pocket'** first. Dig over the area of soil between the paving slabs, removing weeds, roots and stones. Fork in some garden compost.

2 **Plant the blue** irises first, setting them at the back of the planting area – they are the tallest of the plants included. Space them about 45cm (18in) apart since they tend to spread, and firm in well.

3 **Plant the pink** verbascum in front of the irises, spacing them about 30cm (12in) apart. Firm them in. Plant the white rock-cress in front of the verbascums. Water the whole bed thoroughly.

4 **Line the pots** with broken crocks. Half-fill with compost, then plant – put the white *Convolvulus cneorum* in one pot and the African daisies in another. Firm in and top up with compost. Water well.

5 **Place the pots** around the planting 'pocket', then arrange handfuls of pebbles around and between them to give a decorative effect.

Tips
In this type of arrangement it is essential to keep the plants tidy and well-tended – otherwise the whole courtyard can look a mess. Keep the planting 'pocket' weed-free, remove dead flowers and leaves and don't let mould grow on the pots. Water with a fine rose on your watering can so the compost doesn't get splashed onto the patio.

Note
This is a very open, sunny site and the surrounding courtyard paving will reflect heat, so the plants – both those in the ground and in the pots – will tend to dry out quite quickly on hot summer days. Watering is therefore a priority if the plants are to look good throughout the season.

Aftercare
Water the pots and 'pocket' plants regularly, especially in dry weather. Deadhead flowers as they fade.

Triangular Raised Bed

Raised beds give instant height and added interest to a garden and make all jobs – weeding, hoeing, watering, planting and tending – that much easier. The walls must be set on a secure concrete footing if the bed is to last any length of time.

JAN	FEB	MAR
APR	MAY	JUN
JUL	AUG	SEPT
OCT	NOV	DEC

Building a raised bed like this involves concreting and cementing, so you need to allow time for the various elements to dry. It can be carried out at any time of year – weather permitting.

Allow a weekend, for the work.

What you need

Plants

This bed has been planted with a medley of pink and blue flowers – among them alliums, catmint, dianthus, foxgloves, geraniums, lady's mantle, London pride, roses and scabious.

Equipment

Spade, fork, bricklayer's trowel & spirit level.

Bricks – buy single bricks, not pre-cast assemblies – for greater stability.

String and canes.

Wheelbarrow and/or board for concrete.

Watering can or bucket for water.

Bags of ready-mixed concrete.

Bags of ready-mixed mortar.

Sand or gravel for drainage.

Bags of soil-based compost.

1 **Outline the area** and shape the raised bed will occupy using string and canes. The concrete footing will be 15cm (6in) deep, and the first course of bricks will be set 5cm (2in) below ground level for stability. Dig a trench to the correct shape at least 20cm (8in) deep and slightly wider all round than the bricks you are using.

2 **Following the manufacturer's** instructions, make up the ready-mixed concrete in a wheelbarrow or on a board and shovel it into the trench to a depth of 15cm (6in). Try to do this in one session so the concrete sets evenly. Leave the concrete to settle and dry – overnight, or longer depending on the weather.

3 **When the concrete** footing is dry, start bricklaying. Make up the mortar following the manufacturer's instructions (make small quantities if you are unused to bricklaying). Using the bricklayer's trowel, spread a layer of mortar on top of a stretch of the concrete footing. Position the first course of bricks, tapping in and levelling as you go. Complete the whole of the first course in this way.

4 **Lay the second** and any subsequent courses in the same way, overlapping the bricks and interlocking them at corners as you go. Check that the courses are even using the spirit level. Smooth all the joints, striking off excess mortar with the trowel.

5 **When the mortar** has set, fill the bed, starting with a layer of sharp sand or gravel for drainage, and following with plenty of soil-based compost. Plant to suit yourself – flowers, herbs, vegetables and shrubs will all do well in a raised bed like this.

Tip
Using ready-mixed concrete and mortar means the proportion of ingredients is correct right from the start – and you don't have to spend time mixing sand, aggregate and so on.

Note
The more exotic the shape of your bed, the more cutting and shaping of bricks you will have to do. Score along the top of the brick then tap it smartly with the edge of the trowel. Exact shape and size of cut bricks doesn't matter because you can compensate with a thicker or thinner layer of mortar.

Aftercare
Top up the soil in the bed from time to time, and remember to feed the plants in it with a general fertiliser.

Rainbow Fan

Summer annuals are unrivalled for the colour they can bring to the garden – it's no wonder they are so popular for bedding schemes. Here petunias and marigolds have been planted in a rainbow fan of brilliant colour.

JAN	FEB	MAR
APR	MAY	JUN
JUL	AUG	SEPT
OCT	NOV	DEC

Plant in early summer when all danger of frost is past. The bed should flower throughout the summer.

Set aside most of a day for planting – there are a lot of baby plants to put in.

What you need

Plants

Buy bedding strips of purple and blue petunias, yellow and orange Afro-French and French marigolds and variegated-leaf salvias – enough to cover the area you have in mind. Here there are at least 30-40 yellow marigold plants and the same number of orange ones; 20 or so of each colour of petunia; and 20-25 salvias.

Equipment

Fork, spade, rake and trowel.

General-purpose compost.

1 **Bedding schemes like** this do best in full sun, so choose your site carefully. The soil does not have to be particularly rich, but it still needs to be dug over thoroughly. Remove any weeds, roots or stones as you dig. Incorporate a general-purpose compost into the top 8-10cm (3-4in) of soil and rake smooth.

2 **Start planting the** deep orange marigolds at the wide end of the fan. Remove the baby plants from their bedding strip and lay them out in three rows, spacing them about 20cm (8in) apart. Use the trowel to dig small planting holes, setting in and firming each pant methodically in three arcs.

3 **Moving forwards, plant** the bright yellow marigolds in the same way, again in three curving rows. Follow up with the salvias.

4 **Finish with the** two bands of blue and purple petunias, using the same procedure as before to plant them. Water the whole bed thoroughly, using a fine rose on your watering can so you don't dislodge the newly bedded plants.

Tip
To keep the plants producing flowers for as long a period as possible, feed with a high potash liquid fertiliser every couple of weeks.

Note
The salvias are not yet in flower in this bed. They will come into bloom later in the season.

Aftercare
Keep the bed well watered in dry weather. Deadhead faded and withered flowers as often as you can to encourage new ones to appear – and to keep the bedding scheme looking good. Clear the bed in autumn, dig over the ground again and replant the following year.

Cabbages and Calendula

The hot, vibrant colours in this border will light up any garden. Orange and purple is a bold combination, set off to best effect by plenty of green foliage all round.

JAN	FEB	MAR
APR	MAY	JUN
JUL	AUG	SEPT
OCT	NOV	DEC

Plant in early summer for flowering through to autumn. The ornamental cabbages will develop their best colour towards the end of the season.

Planting should take an hour or two.

1 **Pot marigolds and** nasturtiums thrive in poor soil in full sun, so any reasonable garden soil will do for them – there is no need to enrich it with compost. The cabbages, however, like somewhat richer soil, so incorporate some compost in their planting holes.

2 **Prepare the ground** for your marigolds and cabbages by digging it over, removing weeds, roots and stones.

3 **Plant the cabbages** first, spacing them out in the area available. Allow at least 45cm (18in) all round for each cabbage. Dig a planting hole with the trowel, work in some compost at the bottom, then plant the cabbage, firm in and fill in with more compost. Repeat for all the cabbages.

What you need

Plants

Six to ten plants of pot marigold (*Calendula officinalis* variety, such as 'Fiesta Gitana').

Four to six ornamental cabbage plants (*Brassica oleracea* variety).

Two bedding strips of nasturtiums (*Tropaeolum majus* variety).

Equipment

Fork, spade and trowel.
Soil-based compost.

4 Plant the pot marigolds around and among the cabbages, digging a small hole for each one and firming in well as you go.

5 Finally, plant the nasturtiums at each end of the bed, using the same procedure as for the marigolds. Water the whole bed thoroughly.

Tips

The marigolds are annuals and need to be pulled up in autumn, but the cabbages are biennials and will survive through the winter, their colour deepening and darkening all the time as the weather turns colder. They will flower the following year and then die and need replacing.

Notes

If you prefer (and to save money), sow *Calendula* seeds in spring in the place where they are to flower. They will come into bloom in 10-12 weeks from sowing. Nasturtiums are very prone to blackfly attack, which may need to be treated with a systemic insecticide.

Aftercare

Water the bed regularly in dry weather and deadhead the marigolds as often as you can. Remove any broken or damaged leaves from the cabbages.

Nasturtiums Running Riot

In this combination a permanent shrubby perennial – catmint – is planted with a foreground of brightly coloured annual nasturtiums. The two together make an interesting summer partnership.

JAN	FEB	MAR
APR	MAY	JUN
JUL	AUG	SEPT
OCT	NOV	DEC

Plant the catmint in autumn or mid spring and the nasturtiums in late spring. Both will flower in summer.

The time it takes to plant the nasturtiums depends on the size of bed or border you have got.

What you need

Plants	Equipment
Catmint (*Nepeta x faassenii* 'Six Hills Giant').	Fork, spade and trowel.
Nasturtium (*Tropaeolum majus* varieties).	

1 **The catmint is** a permanent planting, so needs to go in first. Neither it nor the nasturtium require rich soil – but they do both like a sunny site. Dig over the planting area, removing weeds, roots and stones.

2 **One catmint can** reach a height and spread of 90cm (3ft) or more, so allow it plenty of room. Dig a hole large enough to take the rootball comfortably, set the plant in and firm up. Fill in with more soil and firm in again. Water well.

3 **Buy the nasturtiums** as bedding strips and plant them as close together as you can for best effect – no more than 15cm (6in) apart. Plant them all round the catmint to form a colourful carpet – they will reach about 30cm (12in) in height. Water in well.

Tip
Nasturtiums flower best on poor sandy soils – if the ground is too rich they will produce leaf at the expense of flowers. Incorporate some sharp sand or grit into the planting area if you think your soil is too rich or heavy.

Notes
Catmint has been given its common name for a good reason – most cats absolutely love it. This affection can take the form of a few surreptitious nibbles from time to time, through pulling or biting away whole stems to full-scale rolling around all over the plant. Keep an eye on your feline if necessary – or take pity on the poor creature and sew it a little sachet stuffed with fresh or dried catmint to play with.

Aftercare
Watch out for and remove any caterpillars you see on the nasturtium leaves – they can eat the leaves down to skeletons if left. Treat blackfly infestation with a systemic insecticide. Cut away any dead or damaged leaves. Water well in dry weather. Clear away the nasturtiums in autumn and dig over the ground ready for spring planting the following year. The catmint looks after itself for most of the year, but benefits from being cut back almost to ground level in spring.

Chequerboard of Herbs

The sheer variety of their leaf shape and colour makes herbs ideal for a formal, decorative bedding scheme – as demonstrated here in this wonderful chequerboard of diamond-shaped herb plots.

JAN	FEB	MAR
APR	MAY	JUN
JUL	AUG	SEPT
OCT	NOV	DEC

Plant in spring for year-round culinary and decorative purposes.

This size of plot may take a day to plant and complete.

What you need

Plants

Clipped and shaped bay tree (*Laurus nobilis*); leaf beet; chives (*Allium schoenoprasum*); curry plant (*Helichrysum italicum*); mint (*Mentha spicata*); variegated lemon balm (*Melissa officinalis*); pot marigold (*Calendula officinalis* variety); thyme (*Thymus serpyllum* variety).

Equipment

Garden spade, fork and trowel

Canes and string.

A number of 15cm (6in) wide, 2.5cm (1in) thick boards for dividing the 'diamond' plots.

Hammer or mallet.

Garden compost with added sharp sand or grit for extra drainage.

1 **Dig over** the entire ground several weeks before you start planting. Fork in some garden compost mixture.

2 **Outline the diamond** shapes using canes and string.

3 **Make divider walls** for the diamond shapes with the boards, tapping them into the soil with a hammer or mallet. Set them deep enough – about 7.5cm (3in) – to be firm and stable.

4 **Plant the bay** tree first, placing it centrally in the diamond at the apex of the arrangement. Dig a hole large enough to accommodate the rootball comfortably. Then plant it to the same depth it was originally in its container. Water well.

5 **Now plant the** other diamonds methodically. The number of plants you need of each type depends on the size of your plot. Here the herbs are: leaf beet under the bay, chives, mint with a surround of curry plant, variegated lemon balm with surrounding pot marigolds and thyme. The plants are set close together to give a tight shape.

6 **Water the entire** bed thoroughly, and keep well watered in dry weather.

Tip

Instead of growing the common mint (or spearmint), try the sweeter apple mint (*Mentha rotundifolia*) which has soft, downy, round leaves and a really beautiful mint scent and flavour that is wonderful with potatoes.

Notes

All these herbs do best in a sunny sheltered site, so choose an open area which gets maximum sun but isn't buffeted by strong winds and is not in a frost pocket. The diamond shapes to the left and right at the front are filled with mineral chippings.

Aftercare

Keep the plants neat and trim by regular picking of the culinary herbs and regular trimming of the non-culinary types. Deadhead flowers and remove any withered or damaged leaves.

Herbs a' Plenty

A profusion of herbs spills out of this bright pink box planter – all highly aromatic and all edible. Position the box as near the kitchen as you can manage so you can help yourself quickly to whatever's needed for the dish of the day.

JAN	FEB	MAR
APR	**MAY**	**JUN**
JUL	AUG	SEPT
OCT	NOV	DEC

Plant in late spring or early summer for cropping regularly throughout the summer.

Allow an hour to plant up this box.

What you need

Plants

One each of the following herbs, bought as young plants: basil (*Ocimum*), dill (*Anethum*), lemon thyme (*Thymus*), lemon balm (*Melissa*), rocket (*Eruca*).

Equipment

Windowbox or planter with drainage holes in the bottom.

Broken crocks for drainage.

Soil-based compost with added sharp sand or grit.

Trowel.

1 **Ensure the box** is clean and dry. Line it with broken crocks for drainage, then half-fill with the compost mix.

2 **Plant the young** herbs as close together as you can, tall ones such as dill at the back, broad-leaved types such as basil, lemon balm and rocket in the centre and smaller ones like thyme at the front.

3 **Top up with** more compost, pushing it between the plants and firming it down.

4 **Hang the planter** in its permanent position, in full sun if possible. Make sure the fixings are strong enough to take the full weight of the planter and its contents. Water thoroughly.

Tips
Get to know the different flavours of the herbs represented here and try them out in different dishes. Basil is the perfect partner for tomatoes and dill does it for fish while lemon balm makes a relaxing herbal tea.

Note
In a planter box as crowded as this, don't try to keep the plants beyond autumn – they will have exhausted themselves in their effort to grow. Discard the old plants and replace with new in spring – either from seed or from young plants.

Aftercare
Water well in dry weather. Crop the leaves regularly to keep the plants trim. Watch out for and remove any slugs, snails or caterpillars.

Container Grown Courgette

One courgette plant in a pot may not seem much, but you'll be amazed at how many gorgeous golden courgettes you can get. Position the container in a sunny, sheltered site, away from strong winds.

JAN	FEB	MAR
APR	MAY	JUN
JUL	AUG	SEPT
OCT	NOV	DEC

Plant in May or June, when all danger of frost is past. Crop in July and August.

Planting should take no more than half an hour.

What you need

Plants

One (or more) yellow courgette plants – such as 'Gold Rush' or 'Golden Zucchini' – bought as pot-grown young plants.

Equipment

Metal container as here – or a terracotta, ceramic or plastic pot – all with holes in the bottom for drainage.

Broken crocks for drainage.

Humus-rich garden compost.

Trowel.

1 Line the container with broken crocks for drainage. Fill with compost.

2 Plant the courgette, firm in well, then top up with more compost as needed. Water thoroughly.

3 Position the container in a sheltered sunny site, away from strong winds which could tear and damage the large leaves.

4 Pick the young courgettes as they grow. This will encourage more to appear, and also the young fruits taste and cook better. Water regularly in dry weather.

Tip

If you have too many courgettes to use in one go, slice them into rounds, blanch in boiling water for two minutes, then cool and pat dry. Pop into polythene bags and freeze.

Note

Courgettes are nothing more than baby marrows – but if you want to grow a whopper for the local show, then choose a marrow variety that is specially bred to grow big. Don't try to force your courgettes to rosette-winning size.

Aftercare

Don't leave the courgettes on the plant too long – they will grow pretty quickly to the size of a marrow, and lose both firmness and flavour. Keep an eye out for slugs – particularly while the plant is young – and remove any you see.

Tiny Tomatoes in Terracotta

1 **Line the containers** with broken crocks for drainage. Three-quarters fill with potting compost.

2 **Plant the tomatoes**, one to a pot, firming them in well and topping up with more compost.

3 **Place the pots** in a sunny, sheltered site – water well.

4 **The tomato compost** needs to be kept just moist at all times. Try to water regularly, little and often – an irregular regime could cause the tomatoes to split. Feed regularly with a liquid tomato fertiliser to ensure consistent development of the fruits.

The taste of a sun-warmed tomato picked straight from the bush is leagues removed from anything you can buy in a shop. Container-growing is easy and you are rewarded with a succession of tasty toms beyond compare.

JAN	FEB	MAR
APR	MAY	JUN
JUL	AUG	SEPT
OCT	NOV	DEC

Pot up young tomato plants in late spring or early summer when all danger from frost is past for cropping throughout the summer.

Planting four to six pots shouldn't take more than an hour.

What you need

Plants

Four to six (or more) young bush tomato plants – a wide range of different varieties is available from garden centres – including red, yellow and even purple ones. 'Red Alert', 'Pixie' and 'Tiny Tim' are all good small-fruited varieties with excellent flavour. 'Roma' is a plum-shaped variety.

Equipment

Terracotta, plastic or ceramic pots with drainage holes in the bottom.

Soil-based potting compost.

Broken crocks for drainage.

Trowel.

Liquid tomato fertiliser.

Tips

As an alternative to pots, try raising tomatoes in growbags – the advantage here is that the bags come complete with just the right soil conditions. You can grow bush or cordon varieties in growbags. Cordons needing staking and you have to pinch out side shoots to restrict the plant to one main central stem.

Notes

For successful tomato growing in containers, make sure you buy an appropriate variety. Check that it is a bush variety AND check that it is suitable for outdoor cultivation – many are bred for growing in greenhouses and won't thrive outside. Take care, too, to choose as sunny and warm a site as possible.

Aftercare

Bush tomato varieties don't need any pinching out of side shoots. Pick the tomatoes as they ripen. If there are still some green tomatoes on the plants when frost seems likely, pick them all and bring them indoors to ripen.

Cabbages to the Fore

There's no hard and fast rule that says the kitchen garden and the flower garden have to be kept separate. You can mix and match successfully as long as soil conditions and site are right – as here in the front of a wide border.

JAN	FEB	MAR
APR	**MAY**	JUN
JUL	AUG	SEPT
OCT	NOV	DEC

For summer cabbages, plant out young plants in May. These will be ready for picking in August.

The time it takes to plant depends on how many you are putting in. Here there are eight or so, which shouldn't take more than half an hour.

What you need

Plants

Eight or more young summer cabbage plants – varieties such as 'Greyhound', 'Hispi', 'Primo' or 'Derby Day' are all suitable.

Equipment

Garden fork and spade.

Trowel.

Soil-testing kit (if needed).

Garden lime (if needed).

1 **Most vegetables do** well on fairly neutral soil, but brassicas such as cabbage prefer an alkaline soil with a pH of about 6.5-7. If you don't know what your garden soil is, buy a testing kit from a garden centre and check. Choose a sunny site sheltered from strong winds.

2 **Dig the ground** for the cabbages several months before planting, incorporating lime, if needed, according to the manufacturer's instructions. Apply a general fertiliser to the soil about a week before planting.

3 **Plant the young** cabbages, spacing them at least 30cm (12in) apart to allow room for growth – check the instructions on the label of the particular variety you have chosen . Firm them in, then water well.

4 **Water well in** periods of dry weather. Apply a regular liquid feed when the heads start to form a ball.

Tips

The soil for cabbages needs to be fertile and humus-rich, but not recently manured. A spot which has had a previous, non-brassica, crop is ideal. Cabbage rootfly can be a serious problem. The adult fly lays eggs near the cabbages and the larvae burrow into the soil to eat the roots – causing the leaves to wilt and stunting growth. To prevent this, fit a 10cm (4in) wide collar of carpet underlay round the stem of each young cabbage as you plant it.

Notes

In this mix and match garden, there are dahlias – grown mainly for cutting for the vase – and sticks ready to support sweet peas. Note that plenty of growing room has been left behind the cabbages. This also allows air to circulate freely, combating rot and leaf discoloration.

Aftercare

Watch out for and remove caterpillars and slugs. Weed around the plants, and firm the cabbages in if they are rocked loose by the wind.

Redcurrant Regiment

Redcurrants have many uses in the kitchen, so it can pay dividends to grow your own. Here single cordons, trained against a slatted fence in a sheltered, sunny position, are producing plenty of luscious summer fruits.

JAN	FEB	MAR
APR	MAY	JUN
JUL	AUG	SEPT
OCT	NOV	DEC

Buy 2-year-old container-grown redcurrants and plant them any time after all danger of frost is past. Fruiting starts from midsummer and continues into late summer, depending on the variety grown.

The 10 or so plants grown against a fence here should take an hour or two to put in.

What you need

Plants

Ten 2-year-old container-grown redcurrant plants – varieties to look for include 'Red Lake', 'Redstart', 'Jonkheer van Tets' and Laxton's No.1'. Redcurrants fruit on short side shoots growing from the main stem so cordon training is a simple procedure.

Equipment

Ten 1.8m (6ft) bamboo canes, plus wires and ties or soft string.

Garden fork and spade.

General-purpose garden compost.

Garden fertiliser.

Secateurs.

1 **Prepare the ground** about a month before planting. Dig it over thoroughly, removing weeds, roots and stones. Fork garden compost into the planting area, then scatter a general fertiliser on top, following the manufacturer's instructions for amounts.

2 **Stretch wires along** the fence at heights of 60cm (2ft) and 1.2m (4ft).

3 **Dig a hole** for each cordon wide enough to take the rootball comfortably, spacing them 45cm (18in) apart. Put a plant in each hole and insert a bamboo cane by each one. Tie the cane to the wires on the fence.

4 **Fill in each** hole with compost and firm in – the old soil mark should be level with the ground surface.

5 **Prune back the** leading shoot of the cordon to half its length, then tie it to the cane with soft string. Trim back sideshoots (laterals) to a bud about 2.5cm (1in) from the main stem. Also cut back to the main stem any side shoots less than 10cm (4in) above the old soil mark.

6 **Tie the leader** to the cane as it grows. In late June cut off all new sideshoots (shoots produced that year) to within four or five leaves of the base. Pick the fruits as they appear – not all currants ripen at the same time.

Tips
When the leading shoot reaches the top of the cane, cut it back to just one bud on the new growth in February. As an alternative to redcurrants, try white currants which are sweeter and less acidic – 'White Versailles' is a popular variety.

Notes
With regular feeding and the correct pruning regime, your redcurrant cordons should fruit well for 10-15 years, or even longer. Expect 1-1½kg (about 2-3lb) of fruit from each cordon. If birds persistently attack your crop, then cover the cordons with netting; do the same if birds such as bullfinches peck at the buds in winter.

Aftercare
Water regularly in dry weather and when the currants start to swell. Keep the soil around the cordons weed-free. In February each year cut back the leading shoot on each cordon to 15cm (6in) of this year's growth. At the same time cut back sideshoots to a bud 2.5cm (1in) from the stem – as you did when planting. In March scatter another application of general fertiliser, water it in, then mulch with garden compost.

Strawberry Hanging Basket

Growing strawberries in a container cuts out much of the hard work associated with cultivation in the ground. The basket is decorative as well as productive and a major benefit is that it reduces slug predation.

JAN	FEB	MAR
APR	MAY	JUN
JUL	AUG	SEPT
OCT	NOV	DEC

Buy young strawberry plants in August or early September and plant straight away for fruiting in June or July, depending on the variety chosen.

Planting a hanging basket should take about an hour.

What you need

Plants

Three or four young strawberry plants – 'Royal Sovereign' or 'Cambridge Favourite' are popular varieties.

Equipment

Hanging basket or terracotta pot (with drainage holes) with chains or hangers and fixings.

Hanging basket liner (plastic, hessian, felt or moulded paper) or broken crocks for drainage.

Potting compost.

Trowel.

1 **Spread the liner** in the hanging basket or line the terracotta pot with crocks for drainage.

2 **Water the strawberry** plants very thoroughly before planting. Half-fill the container with compost. Plant the strawberries in the compost, firming them in well, then top up with more compost. Water well again.

3 **Hang the basket** in a sunny position away from strong winds. Ensure that all fixings are secure and that they can take the weight of the planted basket or pot.

4 **Water regularly, especially** in dry weather. Ensure that water doesn't get on to the ripening berries – this could cause them to rot. Pick the berries as they ripen; this will encourage more to develop. When picking from a hanging basket, don't pull the strawberry – this could tip up the entire basket. Hold the berry in one hand and pick it gently with the other, nipping the stalk between finger and thumb.

Tips

For another crop the following year, remove the strawberry plant from the container, replace the soil with fresh new compost and replant. If birds are likely to be a problem, throw a net over the ripening fruits.

Notes

Check that the variety you buy is suitable for container growing. You don't necessarily want the largest possible fruits in a hanging basket (for reasons of weight), so go for ones with smaller (and possibly sweeter) berries.

Aftercare

Once all the berries have been picked, cut back old runners and remove old and damaged leaves. Cut all leaves back to within 7.5cm (3in) of the crown. If there is a likelihood of frost while the plants are in flower, then protect them overnight with a covering of fleece, netting or newspaper. Alternatively, bring the container under cover.

Brick Border Edging

A neat edging always sets off border plants to advantage – but it can be difficult to maintain. A line of bricks set flush with the lawn makes mowing simple and helps to keep spreading foliage in check.

JAN	FEB	MAR
APR	MAY	JUN
JUL	AUG	SEPT
OCT	NOV	DEC

You can put in brick edging at any time of year, but it's better to choose a dry day for it.

The time it takes will depend on the length of run.

What you need

Plants

The two main plants in this border are lavender and hosta.

Equipment

Engineering bricks.

Sand.

Ready-mixed mortar.

Spade and bricklayer's trowel.

Watering can or bucket for water.

Wheelbarrow or board for mixing mortar.

1 **The bricks can** be laid on a 12.5cm (5in) footing of sand. Assuming your bricks are 7.5cm (3in) thick, you need to dig a trench 20cm (8in) deep. Start by digging the trench along the full length of the border, making it slightly wider than the length of brick you are using.

2 **Line the entire** length of the trench with a 12.5cm (5in) deep layer of sand, tamping it down very firmly.

3 **Make up the** mortar according to the manufacturer's instructions, using either a wheelbarrow or a board for mixing. Lay a stretch of mortar on the sand at the start of the trench and set the first bricks into it, mortaring neatly between each brick.

4 **Continue in this** way for the length of the trench, allowing for any curvature along the way by inserting a slightly wider band of mortar between the bricks on the lawn side of the edging. The brick edging should be flush with the grass edge or very slightly below it.

5 **Leave the mortar** to dry and set before running a mower across the edging.

Tip

Check that all the bricks you use are sound and whole – the wheels of a mower going over them can give quite a battering, which will soon destroy a damaged brick.

Notes

If you prefer you can use concrete instead of sand for the footing – it will be even stronger. Use ready-mixed concrete and follow the manufacturer's instructions for its use.

Aftercare

Lever up and replace any cracked or broken bricks as soon as you can after spotting them. Once there is a break in one brick, those adjacent to it will also start to crumble and disintegrate. Brush dirt, leaves and debris off the brick edging to keep it looking good.

Granite Setts Paving

Make a private little patio corner for yourself – a perfect place to retreat to in the garden for a few quiet moments. A circular area gives a feeling of completeness and repose.

JAN	FEB	MAR
APR	MAY	JUN
JUL	AUG	SEPT
OCT	NOV	DEC

This project can be carried out at any time of year.

Allow 1-2 days to complete the work.

What you need

Plants

A purple/mauve/pink colour theme has been chosen for the planting, with purple-leaved *Heuchera*, mauve-pink thrift (*Armeria maritima*), black Mondo grass (*Ophiopogon planiscapus* 'Nigrescens') and *Aeonium* 'Schwarzkopf'.

A spot planting of scented pink 'Stargazer' lilies makes a bold summer statement.

Equipment

60-100 granite setts.

Builder's sand to cover the patio area to a depth of at least 15cm (6in).

More sand to brush over the complete patio to fill in between setts.

Wheelbarrow, spade, rake, piece of batten, mallet, trowel and garden broom.

1 Measure the area you want to cover (total circumference), then plan out how many granite setts you will need. Order these from a garden centre or builder's merchant.

2 Dig the entire area to a depth of 15cm (6in) PLUS the thickness of the granite setts you are using. Ensure the site is level, firm and solid. Even out any bumps with a spade, then firm the soil by treading.

3 Spread sand over the entire area to a depth of 15cm (6in), then rake it smooth and level.

4 Start laying the outermost rings of setts, butting them up to each other as closely as you can while still maintaining the circular shape. Lay the batten on top as you go and tap the setts into place with the mallet.

5 Continue with the pattern, offsetting each ring of setts slightly for stability and using the same batten and mallet technique. Again, position the setts as close together as you can but not touching.

6 When the pattern is complete, spread a layer of sand on top and brush it into the crevices between the setts with a broom.

7 To complete your secret little corner, make a narrow circular flower bed around the patio – here, garnet-coloured decking has also been installed behind the circular setts area.

Tip
An alternative to granite setts would be a pattern of bricks.

Note
This isn't a patio for heavy usage – if you require a firmer base for your granite setts, then lay a footing of ready-mixed concrete.

Aftercare
If any of the granite setts settle down unevenly, lever them out, adjust the level of sand underneath, then replace. Remove any weeds that spring up in the sand between the setts.

Autumn

If summer represents the garden at its most profuse, then autumn offers a final fling and flourish, with glorious leaf and berry colour and sizzling colours from chrysanthemums, dahlias and hydrangeas.

In autumn you'll be picking your final fruit crops – apples, blackberries, redcurrants – as well as the remaining vegetables. Inevitably, autumn also means tidying up. Leaves must be swept up as they fall and plants prepared for the winter ahead. Think, too, about spring bulbs; don't delay too long in putting them into containers or the ground, ready for a splendid spring display. This season is also suitable for large and small DIY projects. Remember, too, your garden wildlife – make a winter hideaway for hedgehogs and put out food for the birds.

Box of Autumn Delights

Capturing the very essence of early autumn, this box of fiery orange chrysanthemums takes pride of place on a white picket fence and rivals any summer display for colour and richness.

JAN	FEB	MAR
APR	MAY	JUN
JUL	AUG	SEPT
OCT	NOV	DEC

Plant up this box in late summer for flowering throughout September and into October.

It should take about an hour.

What you need

Plants

Two bushy pot-grown chrysanthemum plants – buy them in bud, not fully open, so you get the maximum display in your own garden.

One each of the following plants: Chinese lantern (*Physalis alkekengi*), creeping Jenny (*Lysimachia nummularia*), *Ajania pacifica* 'Desert Flame', sedge (*Carex* 'Evergold') and stonecrop (*Sedum* 'Lemon Ball').

Equipment

Rectangular wooden windowbox or trough, painted pale yellow.

Soil-based potting compost.

Broken crocks for drainage.

Trowel.

1 **Water all the** plants thoroughly the day before you plant them in the box – they are packed in very tightly which means the compost will dry out quickly, so you need to give them the best possible start.

2 **If you have** just painted your container, make sure the paint is absolutely dry before starting to plant. Put a layer of broken crocks in the bottom of the container for drainage, then half-fill with compost.

3 **Plant the chrysanthemums** first, one at each end of the box, checking that their rootballs are at the same depth as they were in their original pots. Firm in.

4 **Place the Chinese** lantern between the chrysanthemums, then insert the four foreground species: from left to right, creeping Jenny, Ajania, sedge and stonecrop. Set each plant in position, then trickle compost on and around the rootballs, covering each one completely and firming in as you go. Use your fingers to push the compost tightly all round the plants. Fill the box with compost to within 4cm (1½in) of the rim.

5 **Hang the box** on the fence, or position it wherever you want the display to be, then water thoroughly. This combination needs full sun to perform at its best.

Tip

When buying the chrysanthemums, don't just pick the first one you see. They can vary considerably in size and quality. Look over all the specimens available, and go for the one with most buds – count them if necessary! It's a simple trick, but it does ensure you get a plant that will literally flower its head off.

Note

Ajania is quite an unusual, sub-shrubby plant that does well in a sunny position. It's sometimes called the 'gold and silver chrysanthemum'. If you can't find one, replace with marigolds.

Aftercare

Don't allow the compost to dry out – keep it just moist to the touch. Deadhead the chrysanthemums as the flowers fade. When the display is over, remove all the plants and plant in the ground – they won't survive more than one season in such a crowded container.

Heather and Pansy Basket

Wow! Here's a sizzling combination of colours. Deep pink and white heathers and velvety rich pansies in a woven-twig basket sing out against a stunning sky blue fence.

JAN	FEB	MAR
APR	MAY	JUN
JUL	AUG	SEPT
OCT	NOV	DEC

Plant in late summer for a long-lasting autumn display.

Planting should take no more than half and hour or so.

What you need

Plants

Three heathers (*Calluna vulgaris* varieties) – one deep pink and two white.

Three purple-pink pansies (*Viola*).

Equipment

Conical woven twig or wicker basket.

Hanging basket liner (plastic, hessian, felt or moulded paper).

Ericaceous compost.

Trowel.

1 **Line the interior** of the basket with the hanging basket liner you have chosen. Prick small holes through if necessary – good drainage is essential.

2 **Half-fill the lined** basket with compost, then plant the heathers, putting the two white ones at the back and the deep pink one in the centre. Firm in.

3 **Plant the three** pansies in front of the heathers, firm them in and top up with more compost.

4 **Hang the finished** basket against a suitable fence or wall – here the relatively simple but intensely coloured combination of plants positively glows against the bright blue fence panels.

Tip

Watch out for slugs and snails on the pansies – particularly in wet weather. Remove any you see.

Notes

Calluna varieties of heather (unlike *Erica* varieties) will not tolerate lime – they must have 'hungry' acid soil. They thrive in full sun and need really good drainage (so don't over-water).

Aftercare

Deadhead the pansy flowerheads as they fade – this will prolong the flowering period by a considerable amount. Both the heathers and the pansies will survive winter if the weather doesn't become too cold. Bring the basket into a more sheltered site if frost is likely. Trim the heathers in spring to keep them neat.

Hot Pink Pots

Hot pink pot 'mums are teamed with sugar pink, purple-leaved busy Lizzies and placed on brick steps in a sunny corner, making a delightful autumn show. Green pots complement the warm pinks of the flowers.

JAN	FEB	MAR
APR	MAY	JUN
JUL	**AUG**	SEPT
OCT	NOV	DEC

Buy bushy pot-grown chrysanthemums and busy Lizzies in bud in late summer for a colourful display in September and into October.

The four pots shown here will take about an hour to complete.

What you need

Plants

Two pots of deep pink pot-grown chrysanthemums.

Two pots of pink, purple-leaved busy Lizzies (*Impatiens*).

Equipment

Selection of ceramic, terracotta or plastic pots of different sizes (here green ceramic) with drainage holes in the bottom.

Soil-based potting compost.

Broken crocks for drainage.

Trowel.

1 **Water the plants** well the day before planting.

2 **Put a layer** of broken crocks into the bottom of each pot for drainage. Half-fill each pot with compost.

3 **Pop each plant** in its original pot onto the compost in the container designated for it to check for the right level, then adjust the amount of compost as needed. Set each plant into its container – the chrysanthemums in the larger pots, the busy Lizzies in the smaller ones. Firm in, then top up with compost to within 4cm (1½in) of the rim. Bump each pot gently against the ground to settle the compost and even it out. Water gently with a fine rose so the buds aren't knocked off the stems.

4 **Both the chrysanthemums** and the busy Lizzies like full sun but can manage partial shade. Here they have been displayed to advantage by simply being placed on ascending steps with a small retinue of 'attendants' – geraniums and variegated sage – at ground level.

Tips

Search second-hand shops, reclamation yards and car-boot sales for unusual or interesting pots. Often the pot can contribute as much as the plant to a display and old ones – as long as they are sound – give an instant, established air to a garden. Cracked or broken pots – usually being sold for a few pennies – are worth buying because they can be broken up and used as drainage crocks.

Note

Busy Lizzies bought for indoor decoration can be put outside from June onwards and left out until the first frosts threaten.

Aftercare

Deadhead the chrysanthemums and busy Lizzies as the flowers wither. Bring the busy Lizzies indoors in the winter – they won't survive outside.

Grey and Purple Profusion

Two-tone plantings always work well – the simplicity of contrasting one colour against another makes for some charming combinations. Here grey and purple late-season flowers create a tranquil grouping in a large stone bowl.

JAN	FEB	MAR
APR	MAY	JUN
JUL	AUG	SEPT
OCT	NOV	DEC

Plant the container in mid to late summer, for flowering until the first frosts of late autumn.

Allow an hour or two – you need to plant the bowl in situ because it will be much too heavy to move once full of soil.

What you need

Plants

Two purple cardoons (*Cynara cardunculus*) – the tall thistle-like plants.

Two mauve-purple floss flowers (*Ageratum houstonianum*).

One each of the following: mealy sage (*Salvia farinacea*); spurge (*Euphorbia myrsinites*); and Swan River daisy (*Brachycome iberidifolia*).

Equipment

Large stone planter bowl (or other container of your choice), with drainage holes in the bottom (this is essential – all these plants must have a well-drained site).

Soil-based compost.

Broken crocks for drainage.

Trowel.

1 **Half-fill the container** with compost. Plant the tall cardoons first, putting them in at the back of the container and firming them in well.

2 **Plant the mealy** sage to one side of the cardoons and the Swan River daisy to the other. As you do this, adjust the level of compost as needed for the individual requirements of each plant. In all cases, the plants should sit in the stone container at the same level as they were in their original pots.

3 **Plant the two** ageratums in front of the cardoons. Then, at the very front, put in the euphorbia. Firm in all the plants, then top up with compost almost to the rim of the container (this is necessary because the ageratums are very low-growing).

4 **Water the whole** ensemble well. All these plants do best in a sunny site and can flower well into October.

Tip

Discreetly stake the cardoons with bamboo canes and soft string if they appear top heavy.

Notes

This stone bowl has been placed against a backdrop of permanent garden plants which subtly complement the purple-grey combination. *Gaura lindheimeri* and *Phormium tenax* provide pink and russet-red accents on the left, while petunias and *Rhodochiton atrosanguineum* offer mauve and wine-red colour behind and on the right.

Aftercare

Deadhead all flowers as they fade. The cardoons and euphorbia are perennial, but the others are annuals (or are best treated as such). Remove the annuals when they have finished flowering and replace with new the following year.

Succulents and Seashells

Succulents are often grown as indoor house plants, but many varieties are perfectly hardy and do well outdoors – if given full sun and really sharp drainage. Striped and whorled seashells make perfect partners for these shapely rosettes.

JAN	FEB	MAR
APR	MAY	JUN
JUL	AUG	SEPT
OCT	NOV	DEC

Plant in spring.

Succulents like these usually flower in June and July but their thick, fleshy leaves provide year-long interest.

Creating a display like this will take one to two hours.

What you need

Plants

Selection of houseleeks (*Sempervivum*) and echeverias – read the plant labels carefully to check that the ones you choose are fully hardy. *Sempervivum arachnoideum, S. tectorum* and *Echeveria elegans* – and their numerous varieties and colour forms – are some to look for.

Equipment

Large stone terracotta or ceramic container with drainage holes at the bottom.

Gritty compost, such as that sold for cacti.

Broken crocks for drainage.

Selection of seashells.

Fine gravel or grit for a topping.

Trowel.

1 **Line the container** with broken crocks for drainage, then fill it nearly full with gritty compost.

2 **Carefully tip the** rosettes out of their pots – the leaves can break off easily, so handle very gently – and plant them in the compost, leaving room for the shells.

3 **Top up the** compost with the fine gravel or grit – allow for at least a 2.5cm (1in) layer. Then pile up the shells around and between the succulents.

4 **Water moderately, then** follow the plant label instructions for subsequent watering. Position the container in full sun and bring into a sheltered area during winter.

Tips

As an alternative to seashells, try pebbles or cobbles of various shapes, sizes and colours. These plants also do really well in rockeries or on the top of drystone walls.

Notes

It can take quite some time for a houseleek or echeveria to flower – and when it does, that rosette dies, but it is quickly replaced by new ones. The leaves of some varieties change colour in summer, turning from green or silvery grey to red or bronzed.

Aftercare

Deadhead flowers as they wither (they usually appear in summer). Remove any withered or damaged leaves.

Hot Spot Hanging Basket

Here's an unusual late-season hanging basket, with plants perfectly suited to their position in a real hot spot – in full sun against a dry wall.

JAN	FEB	MAR
APR	MAY	JUN
JUL	AUG	SEPT
OCT	NOV	DEC

Plant in late summer; the arrangement should last until the beginning of winter.
Planting up will take about an hour.

What you need

Plants

Two plants of bell heather (*Erica Cinerea*).

Thyme (*Thymus serpyllum* variety with variegated leaves).

Stonecrop (*Sedum spathulifolium* 'Purpureum').

Variegated rock-cress (*Arabis ferdinandi-coburgii* 'Variegata').

Dwarf conifer – this is a really tiny spruce (*Picea*).

Equipment

Hanging basket frame, wires and hook.

Hanging basket liner (plastic, hessian, felt or moulded paper).

Gritty ericaceous (acid) compost.

A few stones and/or pebbles.

Fine gravel or grit as a topping.

1 **Insert a thick** layer of liner into the basket – prick small drainage holes through if necessary.

2 **Half-fill the lined** basket with very gritty ericaceous compost – good drainage is essential here.

3 **Plant the dwarf** conifer first, right at the back of the basket. Set the bell heather plants on either side of the conifer, then firm in all three.

4 **Adjust the level** of compost in the basket as needed for the other plants, then plant the thyme on the left and the stonecrop on the right, with the variegated rock-cress in between. Firm in and top up the compost to within 2.5cm (1in) of the rim. Water lightly.

5 **Arrange the stones** and/or pebbles between the plants to give the appearance of a mini-rockery, pushing them into the compost for stability. Finally, spread a 2.5cm (1in) layer of fine gravel or grit on top.

6 **Hang the basket** against the wall on a sturdy hook. The gritty compost and stones and pebbles will make the basket heavy, so ensure that it hangs securely.

Tip
Give the thyme a quick squeeze with your fingers as you pass by for a burst of herby, spicy fragrance.

Notes
The dwarf conifer won't stay 'dwarf' for very long. Check its likely height and spread after five years before buying. These have a terrible habit of turning into giants alarmingly quickly. Remove it from the basket before it gets too big and heavy and plant in the garden.

Aftercare
Water sparingly in dry weather. Clip the heather and thyme in spring to remove straggly growth and to keep the plants neat.

Colchicum Corner

Goblet-shaped colchicum flowers appear in autumn and make a brave show on a patio, in a rockery or at the front of a border. In full sun the flowers open out into wide mauve or purple stars.

JAN	FEB	MAR
APR	MAY	JUN
JUL	AUG	SEPT
OCT	NOV	DEC

Plant in July or August for flowering from September to December.

One 'pocket' of colchicums will take only a few minutes to plant; if you are scattering such pockets all over a paved patio, then time the job accordingly. Broad leaves appear in spring and die back in summer.

What you need

Plants

Three or more corms of *Colchicum autumnale*. (A white variety is available, and also one with double flowers.)

Equipment

Humus-rich compost.
Fine gravel to scatter on top.
Trowel.

1 **Colchicums need fertile,** very free-draining soil and a position in full sun.

2 **Dig over your** planting 'pocket' with a trowel, adding some humus-rich compost to each pocket as you dig.

3 **Plant the corms** 7.5cm (3in) deep and 10-15cm (4-6in) apart, firm them in and cover with more compost. Scatter fine gravel on top – this will assist drainage and help the flowers to avoid becoming mired in mud in heavy rain.

Tip

The stems of colchicum are weak, and the flowers have a tendency to flop in heavy rain; plant them quite close together so they can support each other.

Notes

All parts of this plant are poisonous, so wash your hands after handling them, and don't allow children to pick them.

Aftercare

If the clumps become too congested for their allotted space, lift and divide them in June or July and replant immediately. Colchicum leaves are not particularly attractive, so consider surrounding the planting pockets with pots to hide them.

Nerine and Verbena Border

Nerines provide a final burst of autumn glory in beds and borders with their huge, exotic-looking, rose-pink blooms. Here they are teamed with purple verbena and the feathery fronds of a polypody fern.

JAN	FEB	MAR
APR	MAY	JUN
JUL	AUG	SEPT
OCT	NOV	DEC

Plant the nerines in spring for flowering throughout September and October. Plant the verbena and polypody ferns in summer – the verbena comes into bloom from mid to late summer onwards.

Planting time depends on how big your border is and how many plants you are putting in. A border of the size shown here may take a weekend to prepare.

What you need

Plants

Nerine bowdenii bulbs.

Verbena rigida plants.

Common polypody fern (*Polypodium vulgare* 'Bifidum').

Equipment

Fork or spade.

Trowel.

Gritty compost to aid drainage.

Marker canes, if using.

1 **Nerines need a** site in full sun with very free-draining soil. Dig or fork over the ground they are going to be put into, incorporating some gritty compost.

2 **Set the nerines** into the soil with the tip of the bulbs at or just below the surface of the soil, spacing them about 10-13cm (4-5in) apart. Here, clusters of nerines have been placed along a long narrow border at intervals of about 30-45cm (12-18in).

3 **The strap-like leaves** of nerines appear when the flowers appear – or just after – so there is nothing to mark their presence for a good part of the year. To avoid disturbing the bulbs when you come to plant the other items, mark their positions with canes or sticks.

4 **In summer, plant** the verbena and polypody ferns around and among the nerines, taking care not to disturb the bulbs. This planting serves to hide the long bare stems of the nerines which otherwise look a bit stark – and it also provides a subtle foil for the extravagant blooms.

Tip

If the autumn is very wet, remove slugs and snails which could eat the nerine leaves.

Notes

The verbena is not frost hardy and will die back in winter, but the polypody ferns are evergreen and should carry on. Nerines are relatively hardy, but if you live in a cold area, or if the winter is exceptionally cold, cover them with a mulch of leaf mould or bark.

Aftercare

Cut down the nerine stems when the flowers have withered. Try to leave the area undisturbed – the nerines will multiply profusely on their own if conditions are right.

Gorgeous White and Gold

If you've got space in your garden, go for this magnificent white and gold combination – an informal mixed bed where the plants have been allowed to run riot and do their own splendid thing.

JAN	FEB	MAR
APR	MAY	JUN
JUL	AUG	SEPT
OCT	NOV	DEC

Two perennials – Shasta daisies and button-like *Cotula* – are clustered round a golden-leaved Mexican orange blossom shrub. Plant the shrub any time from spring through to late summer. Plant the daisies and *Cotula* in late spring for flowering through summer and into autumn.

This project doesn't take long to plant but will take a while to become established.

What you need

Plants

Shasta daisies (*Chrysanthemum maximum* 'Wirral Pride').

Mexican orange blossom (*Choisya ternata* 'Sundance').

Cotula species.

Equipment

Spade and fork.

Trowel.

Humus-rich compost to be incorporated into the planting holes.

1 **Choose a site** in full sun if possible – especially important for the shiny, golden yellow colour of the Mexican orange foliage (which turns greenish in shade). Dig or fork over the planting area in spring, clearing away weeds and stones.

2 **Plant the Mexican** orange in a hole that will take the entire rootball comfortably. Fork some humus-rich compost into the bottom of the hole, settle the plant in, and backfill, firming the plant in as you go. Water thoroughly and keep well watered until the plant is properly established.

3 **Plant the Shasta** daisies behind the Mexican orange in the same way: dig holes of the right size, incorporate compost, firm the plants in well and water thoroughly.

4 **Deal with the** *Cotula* plants in the same way, setting them in a wide band in front of the Mexican orange blossom. These will spread quite quickly, so don't worry if you have bare patches between plants at first.

5 **And that's it.** Leave the plants to do their own thing, just trimming back the *Cotula* and the Mexican orange in spring to keep them tidy. Cut down the stems of the daisy to ground level when the flowers have faded.

Tip
The Shasta daisies make excellent cut flowers for a vase, so spare a few for indoors if you can without ruining the outdoor display.

Notes
The Mexican orange can suffer in prolonged periods of cold wind, so place it if possible in a reasonably sheltered area. *Cotula* is an unusual plant. If you can't find it, then try tansy (*Tanacetum vulgare*) or green cotton lavender (*Santolina virens*) instead. Both have finely divided light green aromatic leaves and bright yellow button-like flowers and both are hardy and very free-flowering.

Aftercare
Divide the Shasta daisy clumps every three years or so in early spring. Keep the bed well watered throughout the growing season.

Scarlet and Silver Partners

There are so many flowers available to grow that one can sometimes forget the foliage. Yet some plants offer a leaf display that rivals blooms for dramatic colour and texture – as this superb purple and silver trio demonstrates.

JAN	FEB	MAR
APR	MAY	**JUN**
JUL	AUG	SEPT
OCT	NOV	DEC

Plant all three of these in early summer. The smoke bush produces its best colour – a magnificent rich scarlet – in autumn if placed in a sunny position. The other two are 'ever-grey' and also like full sun.

This is a permanent planting, so you can take as long as you like for it.

What you need

Plants

Smoke bush (*Cotinus coggygria* 'Grace') – rounded, deep purple leaves turning scarlet in autumn.

Several plants of lambs' ears (*Stachys byzantina* 'Big Ears') – soft, oval, woolly grey or silvery leaves.

Several plants of wormwood (*Artemisia* 'Powis Castle') – finely divided, silvery, almost white foliage.

Equipment

Fork or spade.

Trowel.

Secateurs for pruning the smoke bush.

1 You need to establish the smoke bush first. Choose a position in full sun, then dig over the area to eliminate weeds and stones. Don't enrich the soil unless it is extremely poor – none of these plants needs particularly good soil.

2 Dig a hole large enough to take the rootball comfortably. Set the plant in to the same depth as it was in its original pot, then backfill with soil and firm in. Water thoroughly.

3 Plant the lambs' ears and wormwood in the same way, positioning them in front of and around the smoke bush. Allow room for them to spread.

Tips

With most silver or grey-leaved plants, good drainage is essential. Spread a layer of fine gravel or grit under these plants to improve drainage. An alternative, very good grey-leaved shrub to partner with the smoke bush is *Senecio greyi* – this has bright yellow daisy-like flowers in summer which can be removed if you want to focus on the downy blue-grey foliage.

Notes

The smoke bush produces wispy, feathery clouds of pinkish flowers that resemble smoke – hence its name. It's deciduous, so will drop all its leaves in late autumn. The foliage of wormwood is strongly aromatic.

Aftercare

Trim back old and straggly growth on the grey-leaved plants in spring to keep them tidy. Keep the smoke bush to the required shape and size by pruning in spring. Lambs' ears are grown for their silvery foliage, so nip off the flower spikes as they form in summer.

Peppers in Pots

Aubergines and sweet peppers can be grown outdoors in a sunny, sheltered site – choose a south-facing position and put out when all danger of frost is past – you should have the makings of a ratatouille on your own doorstep!

JAN	FEB	MAR
APR	MAY	JUN
JUL	AUG	SEPT
OCT	NOV	DEC

Buy container-grown young plants in May or June for cropping in August and September.

Potting up the small plants will take an hour or so.

What you need

Plants

One each of the following: aubergine 'Short Tom'; hot pepper 'Hungarian Wax'; sweet pepper 'Earliest Sweet Red'. If you can't find these varieties, look for others labelled as suitable for growing outdoors in containers.

Equipment

Three terracotta pots (use plastic or ceramic if you prefer).

Soil-based potting compost.

Broken crocks for drainage.

Trowel.

Bamboo canes for support if needed.

Potassium-rich liquid fertiliser.

1 **Line each of** the three pots with broken crocks for drainage. Half-fill with compost, then check the level of the rootball in each pot by sitting the small plants, still in their original containers, into the pots. The rootball should sit about 4cm (1½in) below the rim of the pot. Adjust the level of the compost accordingly.

2 **Plant the aubergine** and peppers, one to a pot, firm in well, then top up with compost. Water thoroughly.

3 **Place the plants** in a warm, sunny, sheltered spot, away from strong winds and draughts. Water regularly, but don't allow the compost to become sodden. Support with bamboo canes and soft string if the stems start to bend over.

4 **When the fruits** start to appear, water every week with a liquid potassium-rich fertiliser (such as that recommended for tomatoes).

5 **Don't allow the** plants to produce too many fruits – they won't develop to a good size. For plants grown in pots of the size shown here, four or five is the maximum. Once the plant has this number developing, pinch out any further flowers – this will encourage the remaining fruits to grow larger.

Tip

Red peppers are not a separate variety – they are green peppers allowed to remain on the stem until they ripen to a deep red colour. For use in the kitchen, pick them green – the weather in the UK may not be warm enough for outdoor peppers to ripen to red.

Note

Check the plant labels carefully when buying young aubergine and pepper plants – new varieties are always coming on the market, many of them bred especially for outdoor and container growing. Your rate of success will be much higher if you choose the right variety in the first place.

Aftercare

No particular aftercare is required. You will need to buy new young plants every year.

Herbal Elegance

Herbs always do well in pots, whether they are on the kitchen windowsill or, as here, positioned more formally at the edge of a potager (decorative kitchen garden). The tall white pots on a bed of gravel make a striking statement.

JAN	FEB	MAR
APR	MAY	JUN
JUL	AUG	SEPT
OCT	NOV	DEC

Plant the pots in late spring – the herbs will be big enough for regular harvesting from summer right through to mid or even late autumn.

Planting should take an hour or two.

What you need

Plants

From left to right, the herbs in these four white pots are: oregano, mint, thyme with curry plant, and purple-leaved sage with fennel. Buy all of these as small pot-grown plantlets.

Equipment

Four matching display-quality pots with drainage holes in the bottom, plus four plastic or terracotta pots of a size to fit inside the display pots (see Notes, right).

Soil-based potting compost, with added sharp sand or fine grit.

Broken crocks for drainage.

Bricks or wooden battens (see Notes, right).

Trowel.

1 **Insert bricks or** wooden battens into your display pots, then sit the actual planting containers on top to gauge the correct level. The top of the planting pot should come just below the rim of the display pot. Adjust the level of bricks or battens as required.

2 **Line the planting** pots with broken crocks for drainage, then half-fill with the compost/sharp sand mixture.

3 **Plant each herb** in the compost, firming in well and filling up with more compost to within 2.5cm (1in) of the tops of the pots. If you are putting two herbs in one pot, place the taller of the two at the back and the shorter at the front – here, curry plant behind thyme and fennel behind sage. Water all the pots thoroughly.

4 Place the planted-up pots inside the display containers, sitting them on the bricks or battens. Position in full sun – all these herbs do best in a sunny site. Here the white pots are standing on a bed of gravel – this gives extra drainage and also saves the pots from splashing mud in wet weather.

Tips

Curry plant is well named – a VERY strong smell of curry hangs about it at all times – but it is not a culinary herb. Don't use it for cooking – it can be very mildly poisonous if ingested. Remove the flowers as they appear on the culinary herbs to encourage bushiness and leaf growth.

Notes

In this elegant display, the fine white pots are much larger than the herbs actually need; to fill them completely with compost would be extremely expensive – and wasteful. The secret is to pot up the herbs into medium-sized ORDINARY plastic or terracotta containers and stand them inside the larger ones, on bricks or wood battens. The larger pots still need drainage holes – otherwise they stand a good chance of filling up completely in a downpour and flooding the smaller pots. 'Cheating' with the pots in this way also makes them very much easier to move around the garden.

Aftercare
Keep the herbs neat and trim by regularly picking the leaves (of all except the curry plant) for use in the kitchen. Oregano, thyme, sage and curry plant are evergreen; mint and fennel are perennial but will disappear for winter, only to pop up again in spring. Cut back any straggly stems in spring.

Flowers, Fruit and Foliage

Three quite separate elements combine here to give a feast for the eye (as well as the stomach): a deep red mophead hydrangea glows against a background of cream and green variegated foliage – set off by a column of ripe apples ready for picking.

JAN	FEB	MAR
APR	MAY	JUN
JUL	AUG	SEPT
OCT	NOV	DEC

This is an early autumn combination, but the hydrangea can flower from July onwards while the evergreen *Euonymus* has a year-round foliage. The apples ripen in mid autumn.

The apple and the *Euonymus* are well-established here while the hydrangea in its pot can be moved round the garden as needed.

What you need

Plants

Red *Hydrangea* Hortensia variety in a pot.

Apple grown as an upright compact columnar tree.

Shrub *Euonymus radicans* 'Silver Queen' (this can cling to a wall like ivy and makes an exellent backdrop in a border).

Equipment

Large terracotta pot.

Soil-based compost.

Broken crocks for drainage.

Spade and trowel.

Secateurs.

General-purpose fertiliser.

1 *Euonymus radicans* is a hardy shrub which thrives in any reasonably good garden soil. Being variegated, it prefers a sunny site. Buy it as a container-grown plant and position it against a wall or fence where it can cling and climb to form a backdrop for other plants.

2 **The compact columnar** apple tree is designed to be trouble-free. It grows on a single upright stem with almost no side branches, so you don't have to worry about pruning. Plant in well dug ground into which you have incorporated some compost and a scattering of a fertiliser such as bonemeal. Ensure that the rootstock graft (the lumpy bit on the stem) is above ground level. Water the newly planted tree well and keep watering until it is established.

3 **Buy the hydrangea** as a pot-grown shrub. Repot into a larger, more permanent container immediately, using broken crocks for drainage and a soil-based compost. Position where the brilliant flowerheads can be seen to best advantage.

Tip

For a longer display against the variegated *Euonymus*, move a series of container-grown showy bulbs, herbaceous plants or shrubs into position in front of it, starting with daffodils or tulips in spring.

Note

Think long-term for a combination like this – it's not a display that can be achieved in a weekend.

Aftercare

Euonymus: Prune lightly to shape, if required, in May each year. Apple: Feed with more bonemeal in spring. The tree will reach about 2.4m (8ft) high after five years. Hydrangea: Remove the large flowerheads in spring – but not before, since they serve to protect the new leaf shoots throughout winter. At the same time cut back any dead branches.

Blackberry Bonanza

Blackberry and apple pie is one of the great treats in autumn and it's well worth growing your own blackberries. They do well trained against a fence and you can expect high yields from modern varieties.

JAN	FEB	MAR
APR	MAY	JUN
JUL	AUG	SEPT
OCT	NOV	DEC

Container-grown blackberries can be planted at any time of year. The fruit will be ready for picking from August through to early October.

Planting will only take an hour.

What you need

Plants

One or more container-grown thornless blackberry plants.

Equipment

Wooden slatted fence for support, as here – or an arch, trellis against a wall or fence, or a post and wire system.

Secateurs.

Soft string, plant ties or thin wire.

Heavy-duty gardening gloves.

Fork or spade.

Soil-based compost.

General fertiliser such as bonemeal.

1 Blackberries do best in full sun, but will fruit reasonably even in quite dense shade as long as drainage is good and soil fertile. Allow each blackberry plant an area 60cm (2ft) square. Dig over the area thoroughly three or four weeks before planting, incorporating compost as you go. Spread a handful of general fertiliser on top.

2 Water the plant well the day before planting. Dig a hole large enough to take the rootball comfortably. Line the hole with a 10cm (4in) layer of compost, then place the container-grown blackberry plant into the hole – the rootball should be 2.5cm (1in) below the soil after planting. Adjust the level as needed.

3 Remove the plant from its container, taking care not to damage the roots. Place in the planting hole, fill with more compost and firm in, treading down the soil all around the plant. Water generously.

4 Trim the canes to a length of about 25-30cm (10-12in) immediately after planting. This will encourage strong new growth in spring and summer which will produce fruit the following summer after that.

5 Fruit is borne on year-old (last year's) canes. Train new canes up the support as they appear, securing them with string, plant ties or wires and spacing them as widely as possible to promote good air circulation. Water throughout the growing season in dry weather.

6 Your container-grown blackberry will produce fruit two summers after planting. Pick the fruit little and often to encourage the ripening of more. When you have picked all the berries, cut back the fruiting stems to ground level. Don't cut any stems that have not borne fruit – these will produce fruit the following year.

Tip
If the thorns of blackberries put you off growing them, look for a thornless variety – such as 'Loch Ness', 'Merton Thornless' and 'Oregon Thornless'.

Note
A blackberry plant bears long arching canes which can produce 4.5kg (10lb) or more of fruit depending on variety and conditions.

Aftercare
Cut back any dead shoots in February. In spring scatter a handful of general fertiliser around the plant. Then spread a covering of mulch for 45cm (18in) around the plant – use well-rotted manure, bark, leaf mould or peat. With correct treatment and good conditions, the blackberry will fruit happily for 15 or more years.

Build an Edible Border

Growing herbs and vegetables in the garden needn't take up masses of space. This narrow bed, contained inside an edging of angled bricks, enables you to concentrate a number of different edible items in a fairly small area.

JAN	FEB	MAR
APR	MAY	JUN
JUL	AUG	SEPT
OCT	NOV	DEC

Buy seedlings or small plants in pots in spring and plant them straight away. Cropping can start from mid summer and, with repeat plantings, continue into autumn.

Planting will take a couple of hours but this is an ongoing project throughout the season. Building the bed will take a weekend.

What you need

Plants

The plants growing here are: curly kale, lettuce, chives, parsnip and thyme. Make your own selection to suit your own taste.

Equipment

Enough bricks to edge the entire area you want to devote to vegetables – two long sides and two short ends.

Plenty of soil-based or multi-purpose compost.

Spade, fork, rake and trowel.

String and canes, if using.

1 **If you are** starting from scratch – putting your new edible bed in an area of grass or lawn – then begin by marking the outline of the bed using string and canes.

2 **Dig methodically over** the whole area, removing the turf in pieces about 30cm (1ft) square with a spade. Try to take as little of the soil as possible with each square of turf. Once the whole bed is down to bare soil, fork it over, removing weeds, roots and stones.

3 **Still using your** string and canes as guidelines, set the bricks in all round the edge, turning them on their sides at an angle. Wedge them into the soil as tightly as you can – they shouldn't need any sand or cement to hold them in place.

4 **Fill the new** bed with potting compost – the brick edging has the effect of creating a mini raised bed. Fork over the soil again, then rake it smooth.

5 **Now the planting** can begin. Take note of any planting instructions that come with the seedlings or plant pots and act accordingly, spacing the plantlets out with plenty of room to grow. By buying the herbs and vegetables at this stage of their growth, you should be off to a head start with strong, sturdy, disease-free stock.

6 **Water all the** plants thoroughly, and keep well watered throughout the growing season. Weed the plot regularly.

7 **The secret with** vegetable growing is to plant little and often for a succession of crops – why plant 20 lettuces in one go when you can't possibly eat 20 lettuces all reaching the peak of perfection on the same weekend. Grow half a dozen (at most) at a time and keep planting a few every two or three weeks throughout the season.

8 **Once you have** harvested your first crops, replant the area with more – but incorporate more compost every time so the soil doesn't become exhausted.

Tip

An alternative to buying pot-grown plants is to grow them from seed – but for this you ideally should have a greenhouse or cold frame to get the plants off to an early start. Follow the advice given on the seed packets if you wish to take this route to 'growing your own'.

Aftercare
By the end of autumn most of your vegs will have been harvested, though hardy evergreen herbs such as thyme, rosemary and oregano will carry on. Lightly dig over the bare patches in late autumn, then leave until spring.

Garden Still Life

In some situations less is more – as here, where a single specimen plant is set against a trellis screen and complemented by a tranquil arrangement of an ornamental ball water feature and carefully positioned standing stone.

JAN	FEB	MAR
APR	MAY	JUN
JUL	AUG	SEPT
OCT	NOV	DEC

This design can be created at any time of year.

Allow a weekend to complete the arrangement.

What you need

Plants

New Zealand Flax (*Phormium* 'Wings of Gold' or *Phormium cookianum* 'Tricolor').

Equipment

Ornamental ball water feature kit.
Standing stones.
Fine gravel.
Spade and trowel.

1 This small area has been screened off from the rest of the garden by two sides of dark green trellis to give a sense of privacy and tranquillity. All is serene on top, but there's a bit more going on underneath than meets the eye – so a bit of planning is needed. There are four separate elements: the planting; the water feature; the stone uprights; and the gravel surfacing.

2 Deal with the Phormium first – buy it as a container-grown plant. Position it centrally in the angle between the two sides of trellis. Dig a hole large enough to take the rootball comfortably, firm it in, fill with compost and water well.

3 Next, install the water feature. Dig a hole large enough to take the reservoir and pump, then fill with soil around the reservoir to hold it firmly in place. Fill the reservoir with water, put the cover mesh or grille on top, then place the ornamental ball in position, fitting the outlet pipe and fountainhead, and running the electric cable to the nearest socket following the manufacturer's instructions.

4 Position the stone uprights, digging holes deep enough to hold about a quarter of their length securely in the ground. Fill in and firm well.

5 Spread a layer of fine gravel over the entire area to a depth of 2.5-5cm (1-2in).

Tip
You can choose a customized water feature instead of a kit if you prefer. In this case, take advice from the suppliers about installation and running.

Notes
As an alternative, try one of the varieties of Phormium with deep purplish or coppery red sword-shaped leaves – Phormium 'Maori Maiden' or Phormium 'Pink Stripe' are good examples. Both will complement the red-brick edging. Also consider painting the trellis a different colour.

Aftercare
Run the water feature following the manufacturer's instructions – particularly with regard to safe handling of the electrical components. The Phormium is frost hardy in most places, but needs to be kept watered in dry weather. It's evergreen, so looks good even in winter snow.

Thyming it Right

Large expanses of decking can look a little stark in a garden. The answer is to break up the decking with planting pockets or, as very charmingly done here, a ziz-zag edging of thyme.

JAN	FEB	MAR
APR	MAY	JUN
JUL	AUG	SEPT
OCT	NOV	DEC

Thyme is evergreen, which means it has a year-round presence – its aromatic leaves can be picked for use in the kitchen throughout the year. It produces purple flowers in profusion in summer through to autumn. Plant in spring.

Planting takes only minutes, but this will depend on how long a 'run' you require.

What you need

Plants

Enough thyme plants to occupy the area you have in mind. They should be spaced at 15cm (6in) intervals to allow room to spread.

Equipment

Soil-based compost with added sharp sand or small grit.

Trowel.

1 **Thyme is a** hardy – and thrifty – plant and can survive in very little soil. Here it has been planted in an edging bed one decking plank's width in size – in essence, one plank has been left out in the run of decking to make the bed.

2 **Fill the space** left in the decking with the compost – the extra sand or grit will greatly assist drainage, which is a necessity if the thyme is to thrive.

3 **Plant the thyme,** spreading out the roots as much as possible in the space allowed. Set the plants about 15cm (6in) apart. Firm in and water thoroughly.

Tip

When watering – which should only be necessary in extremely dry weather – use a rose with a narrow head so you don't water half the decking as well. This will help to prolong the life of the decking.

Notes

Thyme comes in a surprising number of different forms. There are variegated leaf varieties as well as light green, dark green, silver, golden and even purplish ones, and many of them have intriguingly different scents (lemon, ginger, pineapple etc). Why not try mixing a few different ones together for a patterned effect?

Aftercare

Lightly clip the thyme in spring to keep it in shape and to get rid of straggly shoots.

Hedgehog Hideaway

Hedgehogs spend the winter months hibernating, curled up asleep in an out-of-the-way corner. They do good work in the garden by eliminating slugs and snails – so repay the debt by providing them with a safe, purpose-built home.

JAN	FEB	MAR
APR	MAY	JUN
JUL	AUG	**SEPT**
OCT	NOV	DEC

This can be made at any time of year, but needs to be ready in early autumn for the hedgehogs to find before they settle for their winter sleep.

Allow a couple of hours, depending on your woodworking skills.

What you need

Equipment

For the box: Six pieces of 1cm (½in) thick untreated plywood – two 30cm x 31cm (12in x 12½in) side pieces; three 53cm x 30cm (21in x 12in) pieces for the bottom, back and front and one 56cm x 30cm (22in x 12in) piece for a fixed roof or one 58cm x 33cm (23in x 13in) for a hinged roof.

For the tunnel: two 15cm x 30cm (6in x 12in)pieces of untreated plywood for the sides; two 18cm x 30cm (7in x 12in) pieces for the top and bottom.

Panel pins, 20cm (8in) length of 2.5cm (1in) diameter right-angled ('elbow') plastic piping, wood glue (non-toxic), saw, hammer.

Two or three brass hinges and screws (if using).

Shredded paper and/or straw to line the box.

1 **Make the box** first. Cut six pieces of plywood to the dimensions given on page 144. In the back piece cut a central 2.5cm (1in) diameter ventilation hole about three-quarters of the way up from the bottom – this will eventually take the piece of plastic piping.

2 **Cut a central** hole measuring 18cm (7in)wide by 15cm (6in) high in the bottom of the front piece.

3 **Attach the sides** to the bottom piece of plywood using glue and panel pins. Next attach the back piece in the same way. Hammer in the panel pins as straight as you can for stability. Attach the front piece in the same way.

4 **For the roof** you have a choice. If you want to look inside the box from time to time, then attach it to the back piece using two or three brass hinges. If not, then glue and pin the roof to the box sides, back and front.

5 **Now make the** tunnel. Glue and pin the two sides (the pieces measuring 15cm x 30cm/6in x 12in) to the bottom piece. Then glue and pin the top on.

6 **Insert the piece** of piping in the ventilation hole, with the outside open end facing down so it doesn't get filled with leaves and debris or let water in.

7 **Put some shredded** paper and/or straw into the box so it is warm and snug for the hedgehog, then position it in a sheltered, secluded part of the garden – but not facing north or north-east. If possible, set it against a fence or wall. Insert the tunnel into the entrance hole – and await the arrival of your winter lodger.

Tip

Cover the box with leaves, twigs and branches to give it a more natural look and to help it blend into its surroundings, but take care not to obstruct the entrance or the ventilation hole and pipe.

Notes

Don't use treated plywood – the stain used may be toxic or harmful to the hedgehogs. Try not to look into the box frequently to see if there is someone inside – a hibernating hedgehog should not be disturbed once it is asleep. Also, the less time you spend near the box, the more likely it is that a hedgehog will feel confident enough to take up residence.

Aftercare

The ventilation hole and pipe enable the hedgehog to breathe while it is in the box, and also help to avoid condensation. If you have used hinges for the top of the box, then place a brick on top to keep it firmly closed. Clean out the box once a year in late summer – after the breeding season is over and before hibernation is due to begin. Put some more clean, fresh paper or straw inside.

Make a Rake-Rack

Don't automatically throw out tools when they are past their best. With a bit of imagination new uses can be found for old items – such as this simple yet ingenious tool rack made from the head of a rake.

JAN	FEB	**MAR**
APR	MAY	JUN
JUL	AUG	SEPT
OCT	NOV	DEC

You can make this in a matter of minutes at any time – but possibly choose late autumn or winter when there's not quite so much work to do in the garden.

What you need

Equipment

The head end of an old rake with curved tines (straight tines don't make as good hooks).
Pliers, if needed.
Wire brush.
Strong string or leather thongs.
A large nail and a hammer.

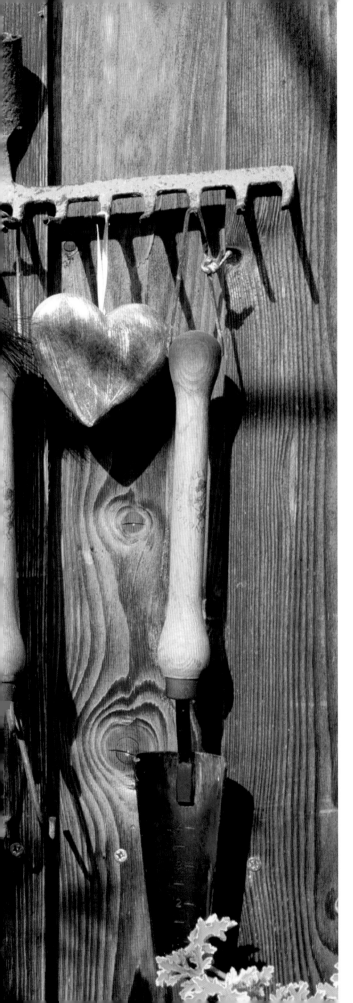

1 **If your old** rake still has the remnants of a wooden handle, then dismantle it by using pliers to pull out the nail(s) holding it together.

2 **Remove any dirt** and loose rust from the rake head with a wire brush.

3 **Nail the rake** head to the door or wall of the garden shed with the tines facing forward.

4 **Thread string or** leather thongs through the handles of your garden tools (drill holes through if necessary), then hang them up on your rake-rack. Job done!

Tips

Make sure you position the rack high enough up to be out of the reach of small children. Also ensure that the rack is nailed securely to the wall and that the fixing can take the weight of five or six tools hanging from it.

Notes

The maker of this rack has indulged in a little bit of whimsy and added a couple of decorative items to liven things up – notably a wooden angel and a silver heart (spare Christmas decorations).

Aftercare

No particular aftercare is needed – just replace the string or leather on the tool handles when it wears through. The rake-rack should be good for many years.

Winter

Winter needn't be a dull grey or brown season in the garden. This is when the evergreens come into their own, along with a select group of winter-flowering plants which can keep interest going right through Christmas and beyond.

When considering 'evergreens' for the winter garden, don't forget that the term covers yellow, grey and purple-leaved plants, as well as variegated ones. With the help of these – and lots of snowdrops – your winter garden won't be bare. And don't forget the birds. In winter, if not before, set up a bird table in the garden and keep it well stocked with peanuts, seeds, bread and cake crumbs, bacon rind and other kitchen scraps. As Christmas draws near, make a traditional wreath for the front door using evergreens from your own garden – and, for a change, try decorating an outdoor Christmas tree.

Wonderful Winter Windowbox

Christmas roses are one of the few flowering plants able to withstand winter temperatures – which makes them ideal for an outdoor winter windowbox. Here they are teamed with conifer twigs, fir cones and gaultheria berries.

JAN	FEB	MAR
APR	MAY	JUN
JUL	AUG	SEPT
OCT	NOV	DEC

Plant your windowbox in late autumn. Christmas roses flower from early winter to early spring.

It shouldn't take more than an hour to complete.

What you need

Plants

Two or three plants of Christmas rose (*Helleborus niger*).

Twigs or small branches of Scots pine.

One or two sprays of wintergreen (*Gaultheria procumbens*) – these bear red berries that persist all winter; buy them from a florist.

Ten or twelve small fir cones and several large ones.

Equipment

Wooden, basket-weave, terracotta or metal windowbox with drainage holes in the bottom.

Potting compost. Broken crocks for drainage. Trowel.

Gingham ribbon and thin bamboo cane or stick.

Artificial 'snow' spray.

Piece of soft thick string and lengths of wire for the fir cone garland.

---

1 **The windowbox here** has been decorated with artificial 'snow' – as has the edge of the windowsill. To do this, lay the box on its side, and spray a thin layer of 'snow' all over the front. Also spray a layer of 'snow' on the windowsill.

2 **Line the container** with broken crocks, then fill three-quarters full with compost. Check the level of the rose rootballs, then plant into the compost, firming in. Add compost to within 4cm (1½in) of the rim. Water in gently.

3 **Now tuck in** the pine twigs and wintergreen sprays all around the Christmas roses, aiming for a 'full' effect. Tie the gingham ribbon in a bow around a thin bamboo cane or stick and tuck it into the front of the display.

4 Attach the small fir cones to the string with short lengths of wire to make a garland, then hook it over the front of the box with bent wires. Place the box in position on the windowsill and arrange the large fir cones in and around it to complete the decorative effect.

Tip
For an extra Christmassy effect, lightly spray the fir cones with artificial 'snow'.

Note
The large creamy white flowers of the Christmas rose will gradually turn a soft pink as they age.

Aftercare
Water the Christmas roses if the weather is dry. Keep a lookout for slugs and snails and pick off any that you see. Dismantle the decorative elements when Christmas is over. In spring lift and divide the Christmas roses if they have become overcrowded, planting them out in the garden in humus-rich moist soil in dappled shade (not full sun). If you want to keep them in the windowbox, water well and feed with a general-purpose fertiliser.

Flowers of the Snow

Though they look so fragile and delicate, snowdrops are tough enough to pop their heads out from a covering of snow – which makes them ideal for winter containers. Here they are partnered with another hardy species – winter aconites.

JAN	FEB	MAR
APR	MAY	JUN
JUL	AUG	SEPT
OCT	NOV	DEC

Plant both the snowdrops and the winter aconites in September. They should come into flower in late December or early January, depending on the weather.

These two little pots will take just half an hour or so to complete.

What you need

Plants

Six to ten snowdrop (*Galanthus nivalis*) bulbs.

Six to ten winter aconite (*Eranthis hyemalis*) tubers.

Equipment

Two terracotta pots.

Potting compost.

Broken crocks for drainage.

Trowel.

1 **Line the pots** with broken crocks for drainage. Fill three-quarters full with potting compost.

2 **Both the snowdrops** and aconites need to be planted about 10-13cm (4-5in) deep. Set the bulbs/tubers in the compost, twisting slightly to firm them in, then cover with more compost.

3 **Leave the pots** in a corner of the garden until shoots begin to poke up through the compost. Then place them where you want the display to be. Don't worry if it snows – the shoots will find their way through!

Tip
Snowdrops do best in partial shade – both they and the winter aconites can be planted out under trees where they will spread and naturalise on their own.

Note
A bonus – and a good reason for having pots of snowdrops near the house – is their delightful scent.

Aftercare
There's no need to water the pots unless the weather is very dry. When the flowers have all withered, lift the plants, divide and replant immediately – either in the ground or in containers with new potting compost.

A Burst of Blooms

Almost anything can be used as a plant container if it holds compost, which means you can indulge your fantasies or eccentricities as much as you want – as witness these magnificent crocuses bursting into bloom from tin cans!

JAN	FEB	MAR
APR	MAY	JUN
JUL	AUG	**SEPT**
OCT	NOV	DEC

Plant crocus corms in September, for flowering as early as January or February.

Here five cans have been planted, which should take about half an hour.

What you need

Plants	Equipment
15 *Crocus vernus* corms.	Five tin cans (or other containers), with at least one hole punched in the bottom.
	Bulb compost and sharp sand.
	Broken crocks for drainage.
	Horticultural grit or gravel for a topping.
	Trowel.

1 **Line each container** with broken crocks for drainage. Mix some sharp sand with the compost, then fill each container three-quarters full with the mixture – crocuses prefer very well drained soil.

2 **The crocus corms** need to be planted about 5cm (2in) deep. Set the corms in the compost, twisting slightly to firm them in, then cover with more compost to about 5cm (2in) from the top of each tin.

3 **Spread a layer** of horticultural grit on top of the compost – this will assist drainage even more.

4 **Set the containers** aside until leaf shoots start to show, then place in position – they look their best when massed together, preferably in a sunny spot.

Tip
This species of crocus comes in lilac, blue, purple and white – so as an alternative buy some of each colour and mix them for a riot of late winter colour on a patio.

Note
For early yellow crocuses, look for *Crocus chrysanthus* varieties – such as 'E.A Bowles' or 'Cream Beauty'.

Aftercare
The crocuses probably won't bloom well for a second year in such small containers, so lift and divide them in autumn, planting them out in the garden where they can naturalise.

Fiery Winter Pot

A few garden shrubs have a special display they reserve for winter – dogwood is a prime example, with bare stems that turn a blazing orange and red colour. Here they contrast spectacularly with delicate pure white snowdrops.

JAN	FEB	MAR
APR	MAY	JUN
JUL	AUG	**SEPT**
OCT	NOV	DEC

The dogwood is a long-term occupant in this pot. Plant the snowdrops in September for a display in January-February. Pot up the dogwood at the same time, or in spring. Included here is a fringe planting of black Mondo grass. Plant it at the same time as the other items.

Allow a couple of hours for the whole pot.

What you need

Plants

20 or more snowdrop (*Galanthus nivalis* 'S. Arnott') bulbs.

Cornus sanguinea 'Midwinter Fire' shrub.

Four to six plants of black Mondo grass (*Ophiopogon planiscapus* 'Nigrescens').

Equipment

Large terracotta pot

Soil-based potting compost.

Broken crocks for drainage.

Trowel.

1 **Place the pot** in the position it is to occupy – a container of this size, once full of compost and plants, will be too heavy to move easily.

2 **Line the pot** with broken crocks for drainage. Fill about half-full, then place the dogwood, in the container it comes in, into the pot to check for level. Adjust the compost as needed, then tip the dogwood out of its container, place it in the terracotta pot, slightly to the back rather than centrally, and firm in with more compost.

3 **The snowdrops need** to be about 10cm (4in) deep, so put these in next at the appropriate level, spreading them all round the dogwood in the centre of the container. Cover with compost.

4 **Finally put in** the black Mondo grasses, setting them all round the edges of the pot to form a fringe falling over the rim.

5 **Top up the** compost to within 4cm (1½in) of the rim of the pot and water in well.

Tip
The colour of the dogwood stems does best – and shows to best advantage – in full sun and can be brilliant when caught in early morning or late afternoon winter sunshine.

Notes
The snowdrops will need to be lifted and divided or replaced every three years or so. For a notable spring and summer display in the container, choose *Cornus alba* 'Elegantissima' which has cream variegated leaves; the stems do not turn quite so bright a colour as the 'Midwinter Fire' variety, but are still an attractive dark red in winter. If you are interested in the *Ophiopogon*, bear in mind that it goes under various different common names – black Mondo grass, black lilyturf and black dragon grass are just three.

Aftercare
The dogwood has attractive mid green leaves which turn orange-red before falling in autumn. The brilliantly coloured stems only come into their own in late autumn and winter. To ensure a good display, the stems must be hard pruned in spring – cut to within 7.5cm-10cm (3-4in) in March. The black Mondo grass bears tiny spikes of pinkish white flowers in summer.

All Spruced up for Christmas

Decorated Christmas trees indoors are a marvellous sight – but for a change why not try an outdoor tree in a container. It will look pretty in the garden and will grow for many years – and you won't have a carpet of fallen needles to sweep up!

JAN	FEB	MAR
APR	MAY	JUN
JUL	AUG	SEPT
OCT	NOV	**DEC**

A small conifer like this can be bought and potted up at any time of year. Decorate as you would for an indoor Christmas tree.

Potting will take up to one hour.

What you need

Plants

Small blue spruce tree (or any other conifer of your choice).

Equipment

Large plastic pot with drainage holes.
Basket big enough to hold the plastic pot.
Soil-based compost to fill.
Broken crocks for drainage.
Moss to tuck around the top of the pot.
Christmas decorations.

1 **Line the plastic** pot with broken crocks for drainage, then fill about half-full with compost.

2 **Ascertain the correct** level for the tree by placing it in its original pot in the new container. Adjust the level of the compost accordingly, then plant the tree, firming it in very securely and covering with compost to within 4cm (1½in) from the top of the container. Water thoroughly.

3 **The tree can** now stand in a suitable site as it is until Christmas. At Christmas time, put it into the large basket and position it where it can be seen easily. Arrange a layer of moss on top of the compost.

4 **Decorate the tree** to your liking – a few well chosen decorations are better for an outdoor tree like this than a mass of tinsel and baubles.

Tip

Choose a stiff-needled variety of conifer – such as any of the spruces or pines – for this exercise. Soft-needled types such as juniper or cypress won't hold decorations very well.

Note

A plastic – rather than terracotta – pot is recommended in order to keep the weight of the ensemble down. This is important since you will probably be moving the pot around the garden from time to time.

Aftercare

Keep the tree well watered at all times – this is especially important for young conifers which have a tendency to dry out quickly. Bear in mind that the tree will eventually outgrow its container; plant it in the garden before it gets too big to handle comfortably.

Front Door Foliage

Here, trailing ivy and cypresses in a windowbox and a clipped, container-grown conifer are joined by a door wreath – all three are given a little extra decoration to brighten them up for Christmas.

1 **For the large** conifer, line the terracotta pot with crocks, half-fill with compost, then plant the conifer, setting it into the pot to the same level as it was in its original container. Firm in well, top up with compost, water thoroughly and position by the front door.

2 **Plant the windowbox** in the same way, lining it with crocks for drainage, then filling with compost. Plant the small cypresses first, then put in the trailing ivy on each side and between the conifers. Top up with compost, water well and position in front of the window.

3 **To make the** wreath, weave the evergreen branches into the wreath ring, tucking in the stems and securing with wire or soft string. Work in this way all round the wreath ring until you have covered it completely.

JAN	FEB	MAR
APR	MAY	JUN
JUL	AUG	SEPT
OCT	NOV	DEC

Plant the windowbox in early autumn. The conifer can be planted at any time of year. Make the wreath in December.

The windowbox and pot will take an hour; the wreath another hour.

What you need

Plants

Three or four trailing variegated ivies (*Hedera helix* variety).

Three dwarf golden cypresses (*Cupressus macrocarpa* 'Goldcrest').

A large pyramidal clipped conifer.

For the wreath, branches from any of the following: *Aucuba japonica*, bay (*Laurus nobilis*), cherry laurel (*Prunus laurocerasus*), *Fatsia japonica*, holly (*Ilex aquifolium*), ivy (*Hedera helix*) or Mexican orange blossom (*Choisya ternata*).

Equipment

Circular wreath ring from a florist or garden centre, soft twine and thin wire.

Windowbox, large terracotta pot, potting compost and broken crocks for drainage.

Trowel.

Christmas decorations, lights and ribbon.

4 Finally, add the decorations. Hang red stars (or other decorations) on the cypresses (ensuring they are not too heavy for the branches). Tie or wire in more red and gold stars on the door wreath, add the red ribbon, and hang it on the door. Wind outdoor Christmas lights through the potted conifer and lead the cable to a safe electric socket. Tuck more gold stars around the base of the potted conifer.

Tips

Here the colour scheme has been kept simple – just green, red and gold. This creates a most attractive Christmassy effect. For a slightly different but equally effective look, try silver decorations. If you buy a large potted conifer, ensure you have at least two people to handle it when you repot it – keep it to shape by clipping in spring.

Notes

The golden cypress is often sold as a very small plant only 30-45cm (12-18in) tall – and at this point it is suitable for containers such as windowboxes. But be warned: it is a fast-growing tree and can eventually reach 6m (20ft) or more in height. It must be transplanted to a suitable site in the garden before it grows too big to handle. The cypress foliage emits a pleasant lemon scent when crushed.

Aftercare

Ensure that the windowbox plants and the potted conifer are kept well watered. Encourage the ivy stems to trail over the front of the windowbox and down the sides.

A Warm Winter Welcome

It's traditional to hang a wreath on the door at Christmas, and there are lots to choose from in the shops – but why not make your own using the abundant and varied foliage and berries available in the winter garden?

JAN	FEB	MAR
APR	MAY	JUN
JUL	AUG	SEPT
OCT	NOV	DEC

To ensure your wreath stays fresh as long as possible, make it as near to Christmas as you can.

It should only take an hour or so.

What you need

Plants

Stems, foliage and berries from as many evergreen plants in the garden as you can muster: here, variegated holly, cypress, ivy (in flower), elaeagnus, rosemary, rose hips and hawthorn berries have all been pressed into use. Aim for long stems and unblemished leaves if possible.

Equipment

Circular wreath ring from a florist or garden centre.

Thin wire.

Soft green string.

1 Start with the evergreen and variegated foliage. Twist and tuck the stems into the wreath ring, securing with wire or soft string. Point them all in one direction to get a 'wheel effect'. Work in this way all round the ring until you have a reasonably full foundation of secure foliage. Space out the variegated or bronze leaves for best effect.

2 Tie small bunches of berries together with wire or string, then tuck them into the ring at intervals in front of the foliage, again securing tightly with wire or string. The berries will be heavier than the foliage, so don't put too many together in one bunch.

3 Hang the wreath on your door using wire or string.

Tip

If red berries simply aren't available in your garden, invest in some really good quality, natural-looking artificial ones and keep them for use from year to year.

Notes

Other evergreen/variegated foliage leaves to try include artemisia, aucuba, choisya, euonymus, pittosporum, senecio and skimmia – as well as all the conifers. Just go into the garden and see what's there!

Aftercare

The wreath should last reasonably well over the Christmas period, but after that the leaves will start to dry up – take it down on Twelfth Night (6 January).

Heathers in a Winter Wonderland

One combination which really comes into its own in winter is the conifer and heather bed, where hardy, brightly coloured low-growing heathers contrast with the upright form and dark foliage of dwarf conifers.

1 **Winter heathers do** best in very well-drained, lime-free soil – so check the soil in your garden, or be prepared to import enough ericaceous soil to build an entire bed. Dig the soil well, incorporating peaty compost as you go.

2 **Plan the layout** of your bed rather carefully. Heathers bought from the garden centre in small pots will eventually reach many times their original spread – these are 'ground-cover' plants. Also, dwarf conifers are not cheap, so you need to budget for how many (and what varieties) you can afford; it is also crucial to take note of their eventual height and spread. This bed has a carpet of heathers spreading out in a wide fan shape on a gently sloping site, with conifers forming a dark green backdrop.

JAN	FEB	MAR
APR	MAY	JUN
JUL	AUG	SEPT
OCT	NOV	DEC

Winter heather flowers from December through to April. The dwarf conifers have a year-round presence, but put on new growth in spring and summer. Plant in late summer to early autumn.

Planting a sizable bed like this will take several weekends – or it can be built up bit by bit.

What you need

Plants	Equipment
Mixed varieties of winter heather (*Erica carnea* and *Calluna vulgaris*) and the slightly taller Darley Dale heath – for example *Erica x darleyensis* 'White Glow'. Dwarf conifers.	Acid soil, with added peaty compost. Fork, spade and trowel.

3 With your plan firmly in mind, start by planting the conifers, setting them into the soil to the same depth as they were in their pots. Water in thoroughly – and keep watering in dry weather until they are fully established.

4 Arrange your heathers, in their pots, around the rest of the bed, spacing them about 50cm (20in) apart; mix and match the different colours until you are satisfied with the arrangement. Plant and firm in, then water thoroughly.

5 Be patient and allow the heathers to spread – in time they will provide an unbroken carpet of colour to brighten the garden all winter long. Neither heathers nor conifers will be bothered by a fall of snow – but do brush off heavy snow from the conifers to avoid breakage of branches.

Tips

Erica CAN tolerate slightly limey soils, but it must be slight; *Calluna* MUST have acid soil. Try to incorporate as much ericaceous/peaty compost as you can at planting time. If your garden soil is very alkaline, consider a container garden featuring heathers and conifers instead of a bed or border.

Notes

A site in full sun will encourage the heathers to bloom profusely. A sloping plot will give improved drainage and a pleasing shape to the bed – you could even include large rocks or stones and make it a rockery bed to echo the look of heather moorland.

Aftercare
Trim the heathers lightly after flowering to keep them neat and bushy. Mulch with extra peat in late spring every year.

Harbingers of Spring

It's always exciting to see the first real flowers of the year – more often than not snowdrops. But hardy cyclamens also come into bloom very early and make a lovely carpet under the nodding white snowdrops.

JAN	FEB	MAR
APR	MAY	JUN
JUL	AUG	SEPT
OCT	NOV	DEC

Cyclamen coum tubers are usually planted from July to September, while snowdrops go in from September to October – so be quick if you want to plant them at the same time. Both flower from December to March. If you plant the cyclamens first, mark them with canes so you can work round them with the snowdrops.

Planting should take an hour or so.

What you need

Plants	Equipment
20-30 tubers of *Cyclamen coum*.	Garden fork and spade.
10-20 bulbs of *Galanthus nivalis*.	Trowel.
	Humus-rich compost.
	Canes for marking, if using.

1 **Dig or fork** over the ground thoroughly, incorporating compost as you go. Both these plants like well-drained, humus-rich, moist soil in light shade.

2 **Plant the cyclamen** tubers smooth side down, putting them 2.5-5cm (1-2in) deep and spacing them 15cm (6in) apart. Firm in, cover with soil and water gently. Mark with canes if necessary.

3 **Plant the snowdrop** bulbs, setting them 10cm (4in) deep and 10cm (4in) apart. Aim to plant them all around the cyclamens but not on top. Again, firm in, cover with soil and water in.

4 **Both snowdrops and** cyclamen spread rapidly on their own – and cyclamen in particular dislike disturbance, so leave them alone to colonise the area as they please.

Tip
Try establishing a mixed colony of snowdrops and cyclamen under deciduous trees or shrubs – the flowers bloom long before the tree comes into leaf.

Note
To fill this area when the snowdrops and cyclamen are not in evidence, put in a spreading herbaceous plant in a suitable gap – wide-leaved hostas are a good choice, or the feathery-leaved *Dicentra spectabilis* with its hanging white or pink 'Dutchman's breeches' flowers.

Aftercare
Deadhead the snowdrops as they fade, but allow the leaves to wither naturally – they will disappear completely by summer. Similarly, the cyclamen will disappear from the scene after flowering. If the snowdrops become congested, lift immediately after flowering, divide them and replant while the leaves are still green.

Making a Pebble Sunray

Here's a really stylish way to enliven a patio – a two-tone pebble sunray which will look good at all seasons of the year and set off surrounding planting to perfection.

JAN	FEB	MAR
APR	MAY	JUN
JUL	AUG	SEPT
OCT	NOV	DEC

This project can be carried out at any time of year.

Set aside a day or two for the job.

What you need

Equipment

200-300 flat white pebbles, 400-500 dark grey pebbles and 40-50 brown pebbles. Order from a garden centre and ask for a range of sizes, from smaller to larger if possible.

Builder's sand to cover the area you are working on to a depth of at least 10cm (4in).

More sand to brush over the completed pebble layout to fill in cracks and crevices.

Wheelbarrow, spade, rake, piece of batten, mallet, trowel and garden broom.

1 **First plan the** area you want to cover, working out how the pebble design will fit into your existing patio. The fan is fitted tightly into – and held together by – surrounding paving slabs. Work out your design on paper – here eight radiating lines of white pebbles alternate with a double 'herringbone' pattern of grey pebbles, with two rows of white at the pointed end, and a final three or so rows of brown pebbles. Note that the pebbles gradually increase in size from the pointed end to the widest part of the sunray. Note also the single brown pebbles inset at the top of each grey 'herringbone'. (You can, of course, make up your own design to fit your own garden space.)

2 **Dig out the** area to be covered to a depth of at least 10cm (4in). Ensure the soil is level, firm and solid. Even out any lumps and bumps with a spade, then compact the soil by treading.

3 **Spread sand over** the entire area to a depth of at least 10cm (4in). Rake it smooth and level.

4 **Begin laying out** the pebbles on the sand, starting with the brown ones at the pointed end. Butt them tightly up against the edges of the paving slabs and bed them in firmly – lay the batten on top of and tap gently with the mallet to wedge them in place.

5 **Next lay the** two curving rows of white pebbles, using the same technique with batten and mallet. Continue in this way with the radiating pattern, starting from one edge of the paving slabs. Bear in mind that it will take a bit of time to match and fit the pebbles precisely – they do need to be fitted together as tightly as possible. The white pebbles are laid straight on their side but the grey ones are angled slightly to make the 'herringbone' pattern.

6 **When your pattern** is complete, spread sand on top and brush it into the crevices with a garden broom.

Tip
Buy more pebbles than you need for the pattern, so you will have a bit of leeway when it comes to matching them against each other.

Note
Since the pebbles are bedded in sand – not cemented in – they should not be subjected to heavy usage.

A Green Winter Corner

If everything in the garden in winter seems to be drab and brown, don't despair. Paint, pots and a carefully positioned bird table can bring colour, life and movement to enliven the dullest winter day.

JAN	FEB	MAR
APR	MAY	JUN
JUL	AUG	SEPT
OCT	NOV	DEC

This arrangement will see you right through the winter and into spring.

Carry out work in autumn. Allow an afternoon.

What you need

Plants

Clipped box shrubs - common box (*Buxus sempervirens*) and a variegated variety such as *Buxus sempervirens* 'Marginata'.

Potted dwarf *Cupressus macrocarpa* conifer.

Ornamental grass in a pot.

Equipment

Four terracotta pots and one chimney pot.

Soil-based potting compost.

Broken crocks for drainage.

Bird table.

Ornamental trellis fencing.

Non-toxic proprietary wood paint.

Brushes and/or paint pads.

Peanut holders for the birds.

Small screw-in hooks.

1 Paint the trellis fencing first. Choose a dry, windless day. Ensure the trellis is clean and dry, then paint using either a brush or a paint pad. You many need to apply several coats to achieve the colour saturation you want. Allow each coat to dry thoroughly before applying the next. Follow the manufacturer's instructions for handling the paint.

2 Paint the bird table in a similar way. Here an attractive paler colour has been chosen to tone with the colour of the background fencing.

3 Pot up the clipped box shrubs in situ – once these are filled and planted they will be very heavy and difficult to move.

4 Place the terracotta chimney stack in position and set the pot of ornamental grass on top. Position the bird table and the other pots in a pleasing arrangement around the bird table.

5 Screw in several hooks around the rim of the bird table, then hang peanut holders, half-coconuts and so on from them. Spread breadcrumbs, birdseed, crushed peanuts and other scraps on to the table – and wait for the birds to arrive.

Tip

Any collection of pots looks better if you can vary the height a little. Here, the terracotta chimney stack gives just the necessary elevation to the ornamental grass.

Notes

There are many different ways of varying this kind of arrangement – the choice depends entirely on your own taste and what you like in the way of colour schemes. This is a quiet, understated corner, with much of the interest coming from the rather charming combination of greens – and the movement of the birds flitting to and fro. The old terracotta pots give an established air to the arrangement which plastic pots (however practical they are) would not impart.

Aftercare

The plants need no particular care over winter – they are evergreen and perfectly hardy. The box bushes will need trimming at least once a year to keep in shape. In wet weather sweep the soggy bird food off the table and wait until the rain stops before putting out more. Replace the peanuts as needed.

Robin's Christmas Dinner

It's vitally important not to forget the birds in your garden in winter – many species rely on our handouts to survive. The bonus is the pleasure it brings to see the birds feeding busily. Here's a novel idea for a fat container to attract robins.

JAN	FEB	MAR
APR	MAY	JUN
JUL	AUG	SEPT
OCT	NOV	DEC

Start putting out containers of fat, mixed with seeds and nuts, in late autumn and carry on throughout the winter.

Making up this container should take about half an hour.

1 Melt the lard in the saucepan but ensure it doesn't boil or burn.

2 Carefully pour the melted fat into your container, then stir in a mixture of birdseed and nuts and mealworms. Put aside to cool and set hard.

3 Attach the hook to the branch of a tree, then hang up your fat container from the handle. Try to site it in a reasonably sheltered area, and make sure the hook can't slide off the branch. It will swing around as the birds land on it, but this won't deter them – and it may help to keep greedy squirrels at bay.

What you need

Equipment

Sturdy metal, ceramic or wooden container with a strong handle.

Large double-ended metal hook.

500g (1lb) lard plus mixed birdseed and nuts – try to find a mixture that contains dried mealworms which are a real favourite of robins. You can even find packets of dried mealworms to mix in with the other ingredients..

Saucepan.

Spoon.

Tips

Fat containers like this are designed to attract the smaller garden birds – tits, robins, sparrows, dunnocks, finches and so on. For larger birds, such as blackbirds and thrushes, put out items like bread, bacon rinds, bruised apples and cake crumbs – but place these some distance away from any fat containers and hanging peanuts so the big birds don't disturb the little ones. This is also important because food on the ground will draw in magpies and crows who are the bullies of the bird world. Don't forget to put out a container of water for the birds, and keep it regularly filled and cleaned.

Note

Don't hang the fat container over any evergreen-foliaged plants or winter flower displays. Inevitably, these will get covered with unsightly droppings as the birds come and go.

Aftercare

When the container is empty – or if you see the birds are having difficulty reaching what's left – take down the container, clean it thoroughly, then refill and hang it out again. If you keep it well stocked, the birds will come to expect it – and flock in for the feast!

Index

Project titles are shown in **bold** type. Plants are indexed under both common and scientific names – as given in the text. Scientific (Latin) names are shown in *italics*. The four seasons are shown in capitals. For fruit and vegetables, look under individual names.